BEING the PARENT
of a PRODIGAL CHILD

Endorsements

Every church has them! What? Fathers and mothers of what we might term 'prodigal' sons and daughters. They took the scriptural command seriously, 'Train up a child in the way that they should go', prayed for them and with them, brought them to church, and exposed them to the glorious gospel of God's free grace. What joy they had felt when that child 'trusted' Christ and began taking the initial steps along the King's Highway' and towards the 'Celestial City.' But then for some reason, they lost their first love and 'backslid', walking no more with the Lord. Like the 'prodigal' they left the 'Father's house' because far off fields deceitfully looked greener.

Author Annie Kirk writes this book with her pen dipped in the ink of her own personal experience as she identifies with the heartache and mental anguish of the prodigal's father in Christ's famous parable. The disappointment that a child isn't walking with the Lord. Battling the fear of 'what if they never come back.' Dealing with the blame game, 'Is it my fault they've left? Could I have done more?' Even sidestepping the temptation to blame God.

Annie determines that this heart-breaking experience is not going to make her bitter; instead, it is going to make her better. Standing at the gate and looking down the road of life praying and waiting for her 'prodigal' to return has not been easy. Having obeyed the command to 'train up a child in the way that they should go', Annie stands firmly knowing that God keeps His promises to every generation. He has never failed to deliver on any of them.

Annie invites readers to think differently about their time in the waiting room of fulfilment. While time spent there can feel like a wilderness and a period of silence, the lessons learned have a purpose and they play a vital role in your walk with God.

Waiting on God's promises to be fulfilled does not mean God has forgotten you and you need to take matters into your own hands. Rather, Annie demonstrates in a powerful way that embracing the silence, being alone with God and resting with Him during the waiting time is the secret to spiritual power, blessing, direction and revelation.

Truly a book of hope and faith for those who are 'parents of a prodigal child.'

David A. Purse
Senior Pastor
Whitewell Metropolitan Tabernacle, Belfast

There are many different types of books. Some you read for education and some are for information. This is a book that will definitely tick both of those boxes. But there is something much more that you will receive when you read it—you will be inspired.

I have known the author for over twenty years and she is the real deal. Her faith is not just an inherited or a cultural thing. It has been forged in some of the painful realities of life that we too often find ourselves having to face. As you read her story you will see that there is no pain that can overcome a person who has received the love of God.

Paul Lloyd
Senior Pastor
Victory Outreach, Manchester Church

This book has been birthed in a time of challenge in knowing who God is in our lives. If we get it right and understand who God is in heaven even we can see who He is individually in our lives as human beings.

When coming to terms with trusting in the Lord no matter where your feet may land or may have already landed; it gives us a place where you never thought you can stand.

Reading this book will certainly help and encourage you along in your journey with God.

Reverend Christie Omodiagbe
Wellspring Church, Watford
Assemblies of God

BEING the PARENT of a PRODIGAL CHILD

God keeps His promises to every generation
He has never failed to deliver on any of them

by
Annie Kirk

Copyright © 2023 by Annie Kirk

All rights reserved. No part of this book may be reproduced or used in any manner without written permission of the copyright owner except for the use of quotations in a book review. For more information, address: annie.kirk103@gmail.com

All scripture quotations, unless otherwise indicated,
are taken from the New King James Version.

Copyright © 1997, 2007, 2014, 2018 by Thomas Nelson,
a division of HarperCollins Christian Publishing Inc.

FIRST EDITION, 2023

Photo by Anna Claire Schellenberg from Thin Spaces Productions
Book design by PublishingPush

Print ISBN: 978-1-80227-971-9
eBook ISBN: 978-1-80227-972-6

Table of Contents

Acknowledgements — ix

Introduction — 1

Chapter 1. Returning to the promises of God — 11

Chapter 2. Hearing the voice of God — 35

Chapter 3. Friends — 59

Chapter 4. Unshakable faith — 73

Chapter 5. Purifying process in the refiner's fire — 95

Chapter 6. Waiting on the fulfilment of the promises — 109

Chapter 7. Lessons — 137

Chapter 8. 'Dark nights of the soul' — 161

Chapter 9. Divine interruptions — 173

Further Reading — 189

Songs — 193

ABBREVIATIONS:

AMP – Amplified Bible

ICB – International Children's Bible

KJV – King James Version

Phillips – J. B. Phillips New Testament

TLB – The Living Bible

TPT – The Passion Translation

Acknowledgements

Family and friends enrich our lives in both the good times and when life can be more challenging. I am grateful to those around me who have contributed to my life and provided inspiration, wisdom and insight. You may not have been aware of doing it but thank you. To those of you who have consistently and faithfully supported and upheld me in prayer, I also want to say thank you. May God bless and reward you richly for your faithfulness.

Having Christian parents and growing up in a Godly home environment helped give me the sure foundation stones I needed to grow and transition from childhood into adolescence and become the person I am today. The quiet example my parents set may never have made headline news, but it has spanned across my lifetime and through into the next generation. Furthermore, it lives on as an example to whoever was fortunate enough to meet, know or be close to my parents.

Becoming a parent myself has been quite a journey. The rollercoaster of emotions never ceases. I am grateful to God for the two beautiful gifts He gave me. Somehow and for some reason, He chose me. He believed in me. He entrusted their lives and care to me. An honour I probably do not deserve.

From the very early days of motherhood, I came to realise that although my role is to care for these beautiful gifts, they are on loan to me because they belong to God. My role is to seek God's will and purpose for them, stand in the gap on their behalf and bring them up as best I can in the things of God. It is also my role to take on that mantel of motherhood and lay the foundation stones to help prepare them for adulthood and the plan God has for their lives.

God gave me a wonderful husband to be by my side in this incredible journey. He is a man who loves God and fully embraces fatherhood despite not having the same role models in his life that I have been privileged to have. He has supported me faithfully in everything I have ever embarked upon. To you, my best friend, I say thank you. I may always be on your mind, but you will forever hold the keys to my heart.

Some answers to prayer would definitely go a long way. The list is long. I know He's working on it. The waiting is hard. Lessons are quality, even life-changing, but nonetheless hard.

If I emerge from this chapter as the person He wants me to be, positioned and ready for the plans He has; it will be worth it all. Till then, the wilderness is a lonely, hard place.

I continue to dream and try to see the bigger picture being weaved. A glimpse is always helpful.

*Remaining faithful in the little is my goal.
One day I will get the much.*

Annie Kirk

Introduction

'Trust in the Lord with all your heart, and lean not on your own understanding; In all your ways acknowledge Him, and He shall direct your paths'.

(Proverbs 3:5-6)

To say that writing a book was never my intention is not strictly accurate. It was on my list of things I would like to do *one* day. Nonetheless, writing a book on this particular topic is a completely different matter and one that I did not foresee. Throughout my life as a Christian, I have had many wonderful encounters and experiences with God. However, these last few years have taken my walk with God to a whole new level. Believe it or not, that new level and closeness with God has come through difficult times. It is truly the beginning of a new chapter into unknown territory, and it is God who has brought me here step-by-step. The storms and fiery trials I have come through, and the lessons learned, are part of the plan God has for my life, and they have a particular purpose. Part of that purpose is to share them with you so that you might be blessed, encouraged and equipped for the days, weeks and months that lie ahead.

The topic of this book is 'Being the parent of a prodigal child.' For a number of reasons, I have deliberately used the word 'child' throughout the text rather than 'son or daughter', 'teenager', or 'young person.' Ensuring the text flows more smoothly for readers is a small part of the reason, but more importantly, the age at which your child or young person goes into or has gone into the far country is not the focal point of the book. Neither does it concentrate on whether you have a prodigal son or a prodigal daughter.

The focus of this book is about your journey with God while your child is in the far country. There are many lessons to be learned during this time and God wants to draw you closer to Himself so that He can speak to you and position you for the future.

Luke's gospel Chapter 15 tells the parable of the lost son and many authors and preachers focus on his experiences whilst in the far country and him coming to his senses. Others emphasize the actions of the father when the prodigal returns home or the attitude and reactions of the elder brother. Less has been said about the father [parent] being left at home during the time that the prodigal is in the far country.

As a Christian parent, the day your child leaves home for the far country and the day they return are two very significant moments in time. The period that elapses in between them can feel like no man's land, a wilderness experience, a dark tunnel with no light and no end in sight. It is a period in time when a parent's life can be hard and somewhat overwhelming in trying to deal with the unknown, contain the fears, anxieties, stress, disappointments, anger, frustrations, embarrassment and the sense of powerlessness and hopelessness. Making sense of it all and trying to analyse and understand what went wrong takes up so much emotional energy. Efforts to continue with and keep family life, church life, employment and everyday routines going and as normal as possible somehow seem a heavier burden than usual.

Such crisis moments and experiences would appear cruel if that is all they were, especially if they were devoid of an overall plan or purpose for our lives. Many times, the work that God does in your life while you are waiting on the fulfilment of His promises, is more important than what you think you are waiting for—your prodigal child to return. Understanding and finding the purpose of such times will ease the sharpness of your circumstances and help you stay focused and stable. If you feel as though you are in no man's land or are going through a wilderness experience ever since your child set off to the far country, this book has been written with you in mind.

I started writing this book while the world was on lockdown with COVID-19. While I wish I could say it was because I had lots of spare time on my hands, nothing could have been further from the truth.

Introduction

Demands from my secular employment and involvement in church life were at their upper limits prior to COVID-19 and lockdown. Since then, both have changed and increased vastly in different directions, each bringing its own new challenges and demands.

Each step in this new chapter of my life calls for greater obedience even when it does not seem to make logical sense. God spoke to me on more than one occasion about this being the time to write. That in itself brought some daunting thoughts, which fluctuated between not knowing what to write, wondering if I could write sufficient material to warrant the contents of a book, contemplating what people might think, and not wanting to appear self-promoting in any way. Furthermore, there is such a vast array of books available on so many topics and in so many different formats. It seems like everyone is writing a book about something, so what could mine possibly bring that would be different from what has gone before? Added to that was the challenge of outwardly expressing some very deep, personal thoughts, emotions and lessons learned—things I would normally prefer to keep to myself.

As I brought all those thoughts before the Lord in prayer, asking for His direction, He replied very clearly to me with Habakkuk 2:2, 'Write down what I show you. Write it clearly on stone tablets so whoever reads it can run to tell others' (ICB). By taking that step of faith and obedience, God promised me Isaiah 55 in return:

'So shall My word be that goes forth from My mouth, it shall not return to Me void, but it shall accomplish what I please, and it shall prosper in the thing for which I sent it' (vs. 11).

Having been left without excuse, I have endeavoured to listen to the voice of God and obediently follow each of His instructions carefully, one step at a time. With each step of obedience has come: a new word of encouragement; repeated confirmation of His promises; enough light for the next step; new courage to keep going on; greater faith and trust in God; and the words to write the next sentence, the next paragraph and the next chapter.

Searching for answers and direction

Everyone has their own preferred sources or go-to place(s) when they are searching for answers or direction. You may prefer to read books written by people who have been through similar situations and learn from their experiences. Alternatively, you may prefer to speak to others and hear first-hand about their journey. Reading your Bible in the pursuit of answers or direction may or may not be something you see of value or relevance in the 21st century. Or, depending on your circumstances, your heart may be so downcast and heavy that it has felt harder to bring yourself to read it.

No matter what your situation is or how hard it is, there are so many powerful lessons in the Bible that God will use to speak to your particular situation. Some lessons may simply be about the faithfulness of God, while others will demonstrate His mighty power to do the impossible and make a way when there is no way. Regardless, each one will lead you on in your journey with God and help you through each and every circumstance. The stories and personal accounts in the Bible span over two thousand years, and they contain consistent key messages that you need to know and be reassured of over and over again, particularly during storms and fiery trials. Some of these messages are simply that: God is faithful; He can be trusted; He has never failed to deliver on any of His promises; God will do what He said He would do; He 'is not a man that He should lie' (Numbers 23:19).

This book aims to fulfil two overarching purposes. Firstly, it aims to re-ignite your passion for the word of God. Through re-engagement with the word of God, I pray you will realise afresh or even for the first time that it contains the answer and direction you need for every situation. Should nothing else come from it, I trust the words it contains will also encourage you to spend time in God's word. Secondly, the book aims to inspire you through the lessons I have learned on my journey. Being the parent of a prodigal child has not been an easy road, but partnering with the Holy Spirit and allowing Him to lead me through difficult days has been a privilege and an honour. Please do remember that this is an account of my journey, and therefore the path God takes you may look completely different from mine.

Chapters 1 and 2 explain in more detail some of the other ways God has spoken to me in the last few years. However, throughout the book, there are references to passages of scripture. These are not intended to be sermons or sermonettes. They are passages of scripture that God led me to at various times, either through reading my Bible or via different sources. I would hasten to add that I did not undertake a search for scriptures on any particular topic when I was looking for answers or direction. Neither did I mention to others the questions or concerns that were going on inside my head at the time. And I am glad now that I did not because I can humbly say that God saw and knew my innermost thoughts, and He brought the scriptures to my attention at precisely the right time when I needed them most. His word truly has been and continues to be 'a lamp to my feet, and a light to my path' (Psalm 119:105). As and when God brought the scriptures to my attention, I started to look more deeply into those particular passages and wrote down the things I observed and the lessons I felt He was showing me. These insights are part of what I feel God wants me to share with you.

'Lord, If You Had Been Here'

We are not always instantly aware or privy to the reasons why things happen in our lives. Understanding and accepting why God does not always respond immediately to our genuine, heartfelt prayers and requests can be confusing. Sadly, our thoughts and attention focus intently on our broken heart, shattered dreams and disappointments to the extent where we wonder why God allowed this to happen in the first place if He loves us as much as He says He does. Often, we do not realise or appreciate that it is in our deepest suffering that we learn the deepest lessons.

I fasted, prayed and earnestly sought God, asking and at times seemingly begging Him to stop my child from going to the far country. There was no doubt in my mind whatsoever that He heard me and He could do it, but it felt like my child was slipping through my hands, and I could not stop it from happening. Neither could I find a reason as to why this was being allowed to happen.

As I was reading through John's gospel one day, I was drawn to the story of Lazarus and his sisters, Mary and Martha. When Lazarus was sick, the sisters sent a message to Jesus saying, 'Lord, behold he whom You love is sick' (Chapter 11:3). Both sisters were convinced that once Jesus received their urgent message, He would come, in time, to heal their brother. Not only did their message carry an urgency, but it also contained a natural anxiousness from the sisters, requesting that Jesus come quickly. That anxiousness was, nonetheless, unintentionally trying to dictate how and when Jesus should restore Lazarus to good health. How naive we can be at times in trying to dictate to Almighty God, creator of the heavens and earth, when and how best to solve our problems!

When Jesus received the message, He did not heed the urgency of the call from Mary and Martha. He stayed where He was for another two days. Jesus had a greater plan which would both glorify His name and cause the disciples to grow in their faith. Meanwhile, Lazarus died, and Jesus tells the disciples, 'I am glad for your sakes that I was not there, that you may believe' (vs. 15).

As the story continues, we read that Martha goes to meet Jesus, and she greets Him with the words, 'Lord, if you had been here, my brother would not have died. But even now I know that whatever You ask of God, God will give you' (vs. 21). A short while later, Mary also goes to meet Jesus and says the same thing. Then she starts to weep. The word 'weep' in the original text is 'klaio', which means uncontainable audible grief. We read that when Jesus saw her tears, He groaned in the spirit and was troubled.

Part of what makes this story interesting is that Mary, Martha and Lazarus all had the privilege of frequently being in the physical presence of Jesus. The virtual sound and tones of His voice was familiar to them. Yet despite that familiarity and closeness, in the middle of her crisis, Martha did not recognise or grasp the words or promises Jesus told her. He talked about 'believing in God', the 'glory of God', and He gave her a promise that her brother would rise again. It is easy to think that things would be different for us if Jesus was standing right in our midst, talking to us. Yet even though that actually was the case for Martha, she still did not fully comprehend what He was saying and thought His words applied to a time in the future.

We can be so guilty of falling into the same trap of missing what God is telling us in our storm or fiery trial. At other times, we do hear Him speaking but we allow the storm or fiery trial to overshadow His words to the extent that it seems impossible they could ever apply to our circumstances, let alone be powerful enough to resolve and overcome them.

Like Mary and Martha, my preference was not to go through this situation. I did not want my child to walk away from the things of God and be caught up in the far country. I, too, wept uncontrollably with grief. Jesus saw my tears and His words to me were that this was part of His plan and purpose for my life and my child's, and it would bring glory to His name.

Getting out of the boat

My uncontrollable grief lasted for a long time but I will explain more about that in Chapters 3 and 6. The fog and heaviness that surrounded me made it hard to see clearly and function wholeheartedly. At times I felt like I was going through the motions. To the onlooker, there was probably no outward difference because the turmoil, screaming and grief were all inside. I felt as though satan was laughing in my face, constantly taunting me that he had plucked my child away from the plans and purposes God had for their life, and he had won this battle despite my earnestness in prayer. Hearing God's voice amongst the others and making sense of it all was initially really difficult.

Storms and fiery trials seem to come either after a move of God or just before He is about to. After being drawn to Matthew 14, I noticed that it was no different for the disciples. Jesus had miraculously fed the five thousand and then He told His disciples to get in the boat and go before Him to Bethsaida while He sent the multitude away. Although the disciples obediently followed the Lord's instructions, they found themselves being tossed about by the wind and the waves. Storms would have been a normal occupational hazard for the disciples who were fishermen but knowing you are following God's instructions and are in the centre of His will makes the whole thing harder to comprehend. Somehow, we assume that obedience means the road ahead will be smooth and easy. It is not unreasonable, therefore, to question whether you have accurately heard from God.

Mark's account tells us Jesus 'saw them straining at rowing, for the wind was against them' and 'He came to them' during the fourth watch of the night, which was between 3:00-6:00 am (Chapter 6:48). What comfort and relief they must have felt when they recognised His voice in the midst of the storm.

God used the next part of the story to speak to and challenge me. Peter asks, 'Lord, if it is You, command me to come to You' (Matthew 14:28). Even with a spontaneous nature and character like Peter's, his motive for getting out of the boat was not to boast afterwards that he had walked on water. Common sense and previous experience would have told him to take cover and head for safety in a storm. So, what possessed Peter to get out of the boat? The storm was not brewing afar off in the distance; it was full-on and up close in Peter's face. He would have felt the impact of the wind blowing the boat and himself all over the place. Peter would have borne the force of the waves crashing over the side of the boat, soaking him and everything else it came in contact with.

I believe Peter wanted to be close to Jesus in the midst of the storm, but that required getting out of the comfort zone of the boat and walking in faith with Jesus. Peter's faith and confidence in Jesus were enough to give him the boldness needed to request permission to get out of the boat. Despite the distractions and fierceness of the storm, hearing the voice of Jesus and seeing Him in the storm made the difference.

The lessons which were reinforced to me through this passage were that I was in the centre of God's will and had been following His instructions. I needed to see Jesus in this storm and know that He was with me. As with Peter, Jesus was bidding me come to Him and be close to Him in the storm. To do that required a ferocious focus solely on Jesus and not on the greatness of the storm or what was going on around me. Facing this storm could not be done in my own strength. By holding on to the

Introduction

word and promises Jesus gave me, listening, waiting and being obedient to His voice, I could not only walk into the face of the storm but also come through it victoriously to the other side. Keeping my eyes and focus on Jesus would mean I can walk on the things that others sink in.

Some lessons can only be learned in the midst of a storm or fiery trial. God uses them to reveal Himself in a miraculous manner. He wants us to understand His deity and mastery over all nature and over every situation. What a wonderful Saviour!

Conclusion

I do not know why you have chosen this book and decided to give it your attention. Maybe you have a prodigal son or daughter and are desperately looking for answers. Or possibly you have finished your last book and are searching for the next title that will capture your attention. Whatever the reason, I hope the story of my journey helps you in some way to find not just what you are looking for but the God who created you. My Saviour and my friend.

This book is not a 'how-to guide for parents of prodigal children.' The lessons I learned became clear to me over a period of time rather than overnight. If you are in a similar season of your life right now, the lessons for you to learn may well be different from mine. The length of the season for you may also be shorter or longer than mine. Be assured of one thing, this season and apparent wilderness are necessary. It is the stepping stone to the next level of your relationship, personal walk with God and chapter of your life. How you choose to use this time 'at home', as a parent, while your child is in the far country, is up to you.

My prayer is that this book will encourage you not only to trust the plan God has for your life but to come to the realisation that God has never failed to deliver on any of His promises. He has never failed me yet, and He will not fail you either. As you read through each chapter, you will find some key consistent messages. Some of these are simply that God loves you and God loves your prodigal child. God has not abandoned you, nor them. He desires to draw close and speak to you. He has not been taken by surprise at what has happened. Neither is He too early nor is He too late. He is and will continue to work all things together for your good. Even when you do not see it, He is working. He never stops working.

I trust that each page of this book will touch you and draw you closer to the heart of God. As you do, you too can hear His voice and begin to understand the season you are in and the purpose of this storm or fiery trial. You can know the supernatural power of God and walk on and through this season of your life with confidence, knowing Jesus will sustain you throughout.

Hard as it may be for you to hear, and indeed believe just now, the message from Jesus to you today is the same as it was to Martha all those years ago. 'If you would believe, you would see the glory of God' (John 11:40).

He is the 'Blessed Controller' of all things (1 Timothy 6:15, Phillips). He has promised. He will do it again!

Chapter 1

Returning to the promises of God

'Let us seize and hold tightly the confession of our hope without wavering, for He who promised is reliable and trustworthy and faithful [to His word]'.

(Hebrews 10:23, AMP)

My world changed one February evening. Everything was going really well, and we were talking and planning things for church one day and the next my child did not want to follow God anymore. I wish I could say that I saw it coming, or that there had been a build-up to it, that something had happened, or someone was to blame. But there was not. I felt like someone had suddenly ripped my child away from me.

Trying to stay focused on my job, continue with church life, trust God with unshakeable faith, and keep my joy and a spring in my step was a big ask. A heavy heart, shattered dreams and a bottomless world arrived on my doorstep even though I had been faithfully loving and serving God. The priority of the moment was calling for me to drop everything else I was involved in and deal with the situation, but that was not an option. It felt like the very foundation stone of my belief in God was being shaken beyond my wildest expectations.

During the days and weeks that followed, I was desperately seeking answers from God. To say that I searched my heart my soul and analysed my actions as a mother is an understatement. I desperately wanted God to show me where I had gone wrong, where I had failed in my role as a mother and Christian parent. I laid my heart and soul bare before God and asked Him to x-ray me inside and out. If there was something in my life that had brought this on, I needed Him to show me and take it away because I did not want it.

As I sought God more earnestly than ever before, He began to speak to me in a new way. It was more intimate and direct than what I had ever known. There were two significant verses that He initially brought to my attention and they sparked the first light in the darkness of my situation. I had read and studied these verses many times before, so they were not new to me.

> *'Beloved, think it not strange concerning the fiery trial which is to try you, as though some strange thing happened unto you'* (1 Peter 4:12, KJV).

> *'In this, you greatly rejoice, though now for a little while, if need be, you have been grieved by various trials, that the genuineness of your faith, being much more precious than gold that perishes, though it is tested by fire, may be found to praise, honour and glory at the revelation of Jesus Christ'* (1 Peter 1:6-7).

Having some confirmation through God's word about what is happening to you helps bring a little understanding and clarity. One of the beautiful things about God is that He does not stop at just telling you what is happening. He has promised that He will never leave you nor forsake you. He also promises that when you go through the waters, they will not overflow you. One of the lessons I have learned is that it is possible to 'experience the most delightful manifestations of His love' right in the middle of a storm or fiery trial (Bridges, 1993, p. 155).

Returning to the promises of God

Remembering and indeed believing the words and promises of God can be challenging in storms and fiery trials. The thoughts spinning around in your head and the promises of God appear to be in an endless battle with each other. Even when you know, believe and stand firm on the promises, these are continually challenged by the visible evidence that your situation does not seem to be changing or improving. The magnitude of the situation before you can make the battle seem hopeless and you feel defeated before you even begin. Thankfully we do not have to be afraid nor dismayed because the battle is not ours. It is the Lord's, and He has never lost a battle yet.

While we all know that God's ways are not our ways, that seems easier to accept for situations that are not so personal to us. For example, who would have thought that marching around Jericho once every day for six days and then on the seventh day, marching around seven times, blowing trumpets and all the people shouting, would bring the walls of that great city down? The law of probability says that battle plan will not work. To the Israelites at the time, such instructions must have seemed ridiculous. Nobody would expect or believe that a shout, no matter how loud, would achieve anything or make the slightest difference. But it was no ordinary shout. It was a shout of faith and a step of obedience based upon a promise that God had given to His people, which made the difference. Most importantly, it was the key to opening the door to the promised land for the Israelites.

God loves to do things in different ways that bring glory to His name. Being obedient to what He tells you to do brings results even when it sounds ridiculous, does not make sense, or you do not understand it. Obedience rather than disobedience is the key. If we could also get our head around the fact that the shout of praise confuses the enemy and precedes our victory, we would not be living under such a heavy defeatist atmosphere and fog of hopelessness.

Coming to terms with the storms and fiery trials we must go through, the way God chooses to work these out and win our battles is beyond human logical thinking. Nonetheless, there is a purpose for it. Going back to the scripture mentioned above in 1 Peter, it is the 'genuineness of faith' that is considered to be more precious than gold, which perishes. So not only will our faith in God be tested in the fire in the same way that gold is to remove the impurities, but our willingness to be obedient is also tested. The purpose of the test is that our faith may be found to praise, honour and glory at the revelation or uncovering [unveiling] of Jesus to an extent which has previously been unknown to us.

What are the promises of God?

There are literally thousands of promises in the Bible, all of which form the basis and foundation stones of our relationship and walk with God. Each promise contains encouraging words to live by in the good times and guiding words for stormy seasons and fiery trials.

The promises of God can be categorized into various themes such as God being with us; the goodness of God; hope; wisdom, guidance and direction; the Holy Spirit; provision; fear; protection; the future; temptation; salvation; marriage, children, family; peace; deliverance; prayer; forgiveness; restoration; healing; resurrection; suffering; and eternal life.[1]

God made promises or covenants with the men and women in the Bible and He fulfilled each one through unusual ways and circumstances that surpass human comprehension. Throughout your Christian walk, God may also have given you promises along the way and you have held onto these over the years. Some promises will be personal and specific to you as an individual, such as 'I will never leave you nor forsake you' (Hebrews 13:5). Others you may have claimed for your family, like Isaiah 54, 'All your children shall be taught by the Lord, And great shall be the peace of your children' (vs. 13). Many promises like Hebrews 13 are ongoing and others like Romans 8, 'all things work together for good to those who love God' may still be awaiting fulfilment (vs. 28).

We are reliant on personal experiences, the accounts of those who have gone before us, and current testimonies, to help build our faith and trust that God is faithful in keeping His word and promises to us. Testaments of God's faithfulness to fulfil His promises are particularly

---

1. https://www.bibleinfo.com/en/topics/bible-promises

Returning to the promises of God

important to draw on during challenging times when it may be more tempting to disbelieve that they apply to this generation or indeed to you as an individual. All the more reason for needing to know or be reminded that God's promises are timeless, and they apply to you as much as they do to anyone who lived before you or will come afterward. Psalm 100:5 is a very heartening reminder that God's promises are neither static in time nor specific to any particular generation.

> *'For Yahweh [the Lord] is always good and ready to receive you. He's so loving that it will amaze you, so kind that it will astound you! And He is famous for His faithfulness toward all. Everyone knows our God can be trusted, for He keeps his promises to every generation!'* (TPT).

Despite the vast range of promises in the scriptures, covering every aspect and season of life—the past, the present and the future—for some reason, they do not seem to be given the priority or attention they were intended to have. Understanding and possessing the promises of God can, of course, only come about when we first know what they are. We have a bad habit of glancing over verses of scripture, not recognising the promises they contain, nor contemplating that they might actually apply to us. We are also guilty of highlighting scriptures, adding a date in the margin and swiftly moving on, forgetting all about them. That is, of course, until we find ourselves in a storm or fiery trial and then we become desperate to hear a word from God and start searching for them.

Our unintentional oversight and lack of knowledge about the promises of God can leave us feeling anchorless, depleted and without hope in a storm or fiery trial. It is time to return to the promises of God but in doing so, we must be careful to ensure they are from God and relate to the storm or fiery trial we are encountering at that specific time. You will know that God has given you a promise or word from Himself regarding your particular storm or fiery trial because He will confirm it to you through different sources.

There is, of course, another scenario whereby you will have received and claimed a promise of God for yourself and/or your loved one. Then along comes a storm or fiery trial which challenges that promise and causes you to doubt. At that point, you may default to wondering whether you did hear accurately from God or question whether He is able to fulfil what He said He would. The longer the storm and fiery trial go on, the harder it can feel to hold on to the promises of God.

Why is it so hard to believe the promises of God?

Many of us have, either intentionally or unintentionally, made and subsequently broken promises to our loved ones, our family or our friends. Likewise, they too have made promises to us, but regardless of their best intentions, some have been heartlessly and painfully broken, time and time again. We have also been let down by people in authority and leadership who we thought and expected to know and act better than they did on the promises they made. The value we put on promises can therefore depend on the reliability and credibility of the person who made them. So, it should be no surprise that we can subconsciously have a very low or no expectation that promises are credible in the first place and will actually be fulfilled.

To add to this, we have not kept all the promises we have made to God and so it would not be unnatural to anticipate the same response from Him in return. Even though God has told us in Hebrews 10 that He is reliable, trustworthy and faithful to keep His promises, it can be harder to believe this without first experiencing it. Not expecting God to keep His promises and/or believing they were never intended for us anyway can seem easier than dealing with the disappointment of another broken promise.

Having control over the promises we make to our children, family or friends and setting a timescale for these sits more comfortably with us. Furthermore, when others make us a promise, if for some reason this does not happen within the set timescale, we generally find out the reason for the delay fairly quickly. God's promises, however, do not come with a set timescale and they most definitely do not match our expectations of when they should be fulfilled. Finding ourselves totally out of control over the timescale for promises to be fulfilled is unsettling. If situations do not change or promises are not fulfilled within a timescale we consider to be reasonable, we quickly become disillusioned with God.

It can also be hard to accept and understand that if God has given us all these promises, and if He is a loving Father, why would He allow us to go through such heartbreaking situations which challenge their authenticity. As a parent, we try everything we can within our power to give our children the things they want or need. Where possible, we also try to make things go as smoothly as possible to prevent them from disappointments and heartache. Some of us have even been guilty of maneuvering and manipulating situations when our children were younger to ensure they work out in a way we think is best for them. Needless to say, that is not the case with Almighty God, and so we become frustrated when life is not plain sailing. We assume we have got it wrong concerning the promises of God and begin doubting they were ever applicable to us in the first place. The seemingly apparent mixed messages between the promises of God and storms or fiery trials can be confusing.

Watching your prodigal child heading down the wrong road, making terrible decisions despite all the things you have tried to teach them growing up, is extremely difficult. Not only are you out of control of the decisions they are making, but you must also relinquish control of their life to God, not knowing the overall plan and timescale He has for them. In the absence of visible changes or measurable progress, the promises of God that you have for your child look unlikely to ever come to fruition and so once again, you begin questioning their accuracy. Believing and holding on to the promises of God for your child no longer seems relevant because they do not match what is being played out in reality before your very eyes. In our desperation and desire to prevent our prodigal child from this collision course with disaster, along with our need to try and control the situation, we offer suggestions and options to God on how He could solve our situation and fulfil the promises! But when He does not do it our way, we become upset, fall out with Him, stop praying and put the promises to one side.

Waiting on the fulfilment of God's promises is one of the hardest things for a Christian to do. We can and should take courage from knowing that we are not the only generation of people who have had to wait for God's promises and plans to be fulfilled in our lives, but we do not. Genesis 37 tells the story of how Joseph waited thirteen years for his dream to be fulfilled. Abraham waited twenty-five years for Isaac to be born (Genesis 21). Moses waited forty years to bring the Israelites out of Egypt (Exodus} and David waited between fifteen and twenty years to become king of Israel after being anointed for the role (2 Samuel 2).

The waiting time does not get any easier even though we know that 'tribulation produces perseverance; and perseverance, character and character, hope' (Romans 5:3-4). We can and should, however, take comfort in knowing that God has a perfect plan for us and that His timing is perfect. Sadly, we do not do that either. Galatians 4 talks about the 'fullness of time' or 'when [in God's plan] the proper time had fully come' (vs. 4, AMP). Waiting on the promises to be fulfilled does not mean that God has forgotten about you. His ways and timings far exceed human understanding. Despite knowing that, our belief in the promises of God can at times lose momentum while we are in the waiting room of fulfilment.

The longer your child is in the far country, the easier it is to believe the promises were not from God and do not relate to your situation. Attempts to try and find answers and direction can draw you towards other people's testimonies about God's faithfulness in fulfilling His promises. While that can be helpful, somehow, the path to their answered prayer and fulfilled promises seems to be much quicker and easier! It is almost as though they found a shortcut through their storm or fiery trial. Neither do they appear to have flinched at the wind of adversity that has suddenly come upon them. Understandably, their stories and testimonies generally only contain the highlights. While that is reasonable because of time constraints, quite often, we miss out on hearing what God did in their life during that time, how they kept going and got from one point to another and the lessons they learned along the way. Of course, testimonies can and do bring encouragement and a ray of hope that if God can do it for them, He can do it for you and your prodigal child. Nonetheless, testimonies can carry a risk of being presented seamlessly and victoriously. They can make it appear that no one else has had the same emotional rollercoaster experience, doubts or internal battles you are going through. Thinking that it must just be you who is handling the situation wrongly is an easy assumption and conclusion to arrive at.

Believing the promises of God is also hard when answers to prayer seem to be delayed and the wind of adversity continues to blow strong in your face. In actual fact, nothing could be further from the truth because there is an appointed length of time for the storm or fiery trial you are in. It will not last one moment longer than God intended it to in the plan He has for your life. As 2 Peter 3 says, 'The Lord is not slack [does not delay beyond the appointed time] concerning His promise, as some count slackness, but is longsuffering toward us, not willing that any should perish but that all should come to repentance' (vs. 9).

Do you believe the promises of God?

Believing the promises of God and that He is faithful to keep them, even when you cannot see any visible signs of fulfilment, requires you to live and walk by faith rather than sight. How easy it is to verbally say you believe God will fulfil His promises to you but do you really believe it in your heart? If God's promises were answered quickly, then, of course, you would not hesitate to say you believe. Having to wait on the promises often without any indication of change or positive progress can cause seeds of doubt to enter your mind. It is not long thereafter before these seeds of doubt grow and manifest into something bigger.

Knowing that the Lord desires 'truth in the inward parts', I began to search my own heart and life to see if there was anything hindering the promises of God from being fulfilled. My desire was for that clean and pure heart that the Psalmist talks about and for God to deal with anything that was not right. One of the first things I felt the Holy Spirit challenge me on was 'Do you really believe the promises of God are for you?' My answer was undoubtedly yes. However, this belief did not align with the grief and heaviness I felt inside.

During worship at church one Sunday morning, we were singing the song below called 'With All I am'.[i]

> *'Into Your hand, I commit again*
> *With All I am for You Lord*
> *You hold my world in the palm of Your hand*
> *And I am Yours, forever*
>
> *Jesus, I believe in You*
> *Jesus, I belong to You*
> *You're the reason that I live, The reason that I sing*
> *With all I am*
>
> *I will walk with You, Wherever You go*
> *Through tears and joy, I will trust in You*
> *And I will live, In all of Your ways*
> *Your promises forever*
>
> *I will worship*
> *I will worship You*
> *I will worship*
> *I will worship You'.*

On this particular morning, I could sense the nearness of the Holy Spirit and I heard that still small voice whisper in my ear, 'Do I hold your world and your child's in the palm of my hand?' My silent answer was, 'yes, Lord, you do'. His response was simply, 'Well, why are you so anxious? Why are you trying to take back control of the situation?'

As we continued to sing the song, I also felt the Holy Spirit challenge me over the words 'I will worship'. He showed me that this was something I had to make a choice over. I could either declare that I was going to worship the Lord regardless of my situation, or I could choose to allow the heaviness and the grief to pull me down. The truth of the matter is that it is easier to trust God when everything is going well but harder to do so through tears and disappointments.

Both the lyrics in a song and the melody can be very powerful and a real blessing as we worship and praise the Lord. But sometimes, we are less aware that we are actually singing about the promises of God and declaring our response to them. Despite our playlists being on repeat, we may never stop and challenge ourselves over whether we actually believe what we are singing. Maybe it is time to stop asking God why is this being allowed to happen to me and start asking questions like 'Lord, what do you want to do in my life at this time while my prodigal child is in the far country?' Or 'Lord, how do you want to change and position me for the future to bring glory to your name?'

Challenging the doubts

While you cannot stop recurring thoughts about whether God is faithful to keep His promises from trying to seep into your mind, you can choose how to respond. Do not lose sight of the fact that He always keeps His word and He is clear about this in the scriptures, especially when He says, 'No, I will not break my covenant; I will not take back one word of what I said' (Psalm 89:34, TLB). We also know that 'not one word of all the good words which the LORD your God has promised concerning you has failed; all have been fulfilled for you, not one of them has failed' (Joshua 23:14, AMP). From generation to generation right throughout history, God has demonstrated that He is faithful to His word and is trustworthy. It would be extremely foolish of us in this generation to think that had somehow changed.

Making a purposeful decision to believe in the promises of God and trust that you are going to come out of this storm differently and closer to God is really important. You are the victor in your storm rather than the victim, no matter what your situation looks like. Knowing and believing this will help you to get through each day and overcome the voice of the enemy that would try to tell you otherwise.

Accepting and trusting that God is still in control even when bad things happen to good people, namely your child, is undoubtedly difficult. When those seeds of doubt do come into your head, there is no better place to look than the word of God to find out how others coped in their storms and learn from them. Daniel Chapter 1, for example, tells the story of how Nebuchadnezzar, king of Babylon, besieged Jerusalem.

He 'instructed Ashpenaz, master of his eunuchs, to bring some of the children of Israel and some of the king's descendants and some of the nobles, young men in whom there was no blemish, but good-looking, gifted in all wisdom, possessing knowledge and quick to understand, who had the ability to serve in the king's palace, and whom they might teach the language and literature of the Chaldeans' (vs. 3-4).

The criteria which the Babylonian king gave to select these young men was a tall order. They were to be 'comely [pleasant to look at] and well-favoured, whose countenances [faces] were indexes [signs] of ingenuity [clever, original, inventive] and good humour.... they must be skilful in all wisdom, and cunning, or well-seen in knowledge and understanding science, such as were quick and sharp and could give a ready and intelligent account of their own country and of the learning they had hitherto been brought up in' (Henry, 1992, p. 1428). Daniel and his three friends Hananiah, Mishael and Azariah met these criteria and were among the 3023 who were captured and taken from their family and homes in Jerusalem to Babylon, some 500 plus miles away.

Comprehending what the parents of these young men [aged 16 approximately] must have gone through is very difficult. Their sons, whom they loved and nurtured, were cruelly wrenched away from them at such a tender and influential age. Arrangements that would already have been put in place for their future were destroyed, and they were taken to a foreign land, a place where their destiny was unknown.

In an attempt to show authority over the young men and 'naturalise' them, the prince of the eunuchs changed their names from something that had references about God to names that savoured Chaldean idolatry. Daniel which means 'God is my judge', became Belteshazzar. Hananiah, which means 'the grace of the Lord', became Shadrach. Mishael, which means 'He that is the strong God', became Meshach. Azariah, meaning 'The Lord is a help', became Abed-Nego. The prince could change their names, but he could not change their nature or identity.

The sadness and cruelty of this situation make it hard to see God's hand in it. Yet everything that happened to Daniel and his friends was the Lord's doing. The Babylonian captivity was foretold by Jeremiah through prophecy (Chapter 25). Jeremiah even wrote a letter to the exiled com-

Returning to the promises of God

munity reminding them that it was God, not Nebuchadnezzar, who had caused them to be carried away (Chapter 29:4). Babylon was exactly the place where God wanted Daniel and his friends to be, but it was not the experience any parent would have wanted for their child. Neither was Babylon a place where the captives, nor their families, would have chosen for their loved ones.

We can learn so much from Daniel, particularly about his actions during the many challenges he faced and how he coped with his storms and fiery trials. Verse 8 of Chapter 1 says, 'But Daniel purposed in his heart that he would not defile himself with the portion of the king's delicacies nor with the wine which he drank'. As a teenager, Daniel took his stand even when it could have cost him his life. Because of it, God blessed Daniel and brought him 'into the favour and goodwill of the chief of the eunuchs' (vs. 9). Taking his stand in this first trial was a forerunner for some of the future situations that Daniel would find himself having to face through no fault of his own.

Reading Daniel's story makes you wonder what his parents, and those of his friends, were like. What kind of upbringing, Godly teaching and role models did they have in their early years? Whatever they experienced, it must surely have influenced their decision-making processes and encouraged them to completely trust in and have faith that God would be with them in this foreign land during their storms and fiery trials.

God's plan, purpose and destiny were for Daniel and his friends to be powerful influences right in the heart of this idolatrous nation. He was in control of their situation. He never left them. In fact, He blessed them. We read that 'God gave them knowledge and skill in all literature and wisdom, and Daniel had understanding in all visions and dreams' (Chapter 1:17). Everything seemed to be going well and when Daniel interpreted king Nebuchadnezzar's dream, both he and his friends were promoted. Then suddenly, out of nowhere, their situation changed for the worse. Nebuchadnezzar made an image of gold and commanded that everyone was to bow down to it. When Daniel's friends, Shadrach, Meshach and Abed-Nego, refused to do so, certain Chaldeans accused the Jews of not paying due respect to the king and their punishment was to be thrown into the fiery furnace.

How tempting it is to blame the devil when things go wrong in our lives. Here we are doing our best, trying to serve God and do His work, and then something happens which interrupts and thwarts our plans. We do not consider that God could possibly be in control of our situation. Here in this passage of scripture, we can see how Shadrach, Meshach and Abed-Nego's faith was being tried and tested. Giving in and bowing down to the image would have looked like an easier option for them. In fact, no one would have blamed them if faced with the same dilemma. Being in that situation, and indeed looking on from a distance, it probably felt and looked like God had abandoned them in this foreign land and was nowhere to be seen. But God was with them the whole time, including in the fiery furnace. He gave them the courage, boldness and determination to take their stand in the midst of their situation. Look at what God did in and through it—the miraculous power and the glory of Almighty God were publicly demonstrated and the nation was changed.

We celebrate and thank God for getting us through one storm—and rightly so. However, that does not mean that there will not be another one. Each storm is intended to build your faith in preparation for the future plans and purpose God has for you. Daniel encountered many storms and fiery trials throughout his life, even though he was in a position of authority in Babylon. One of the first steps he took in his journey was to 'purpose in his heart'. Whatever role models or sources that Daniel had previously sought advice or counsel from in Jerusalem were gone when he was taken away from there. Daniel had to learn to take his stand, believe, have faith in God for himself and make his own decisions. As he did so, God blessed him and prepared him for the next storm.

Many years later, when Daniel was in his seventies, the governors and satraps plotted against him and managed to get king Darius to sign a decree that anyone who petitioned any god [except himself] in the next 30 days would be cast into the lion's den. Daniel had every right to go into panic mode and blame God for getting him into this predicament. Yet he was undeterred by the royal proclamation and went home and prayed in his room with his windows open toward Jerusalem. Three times that day, he prayed and gave thanks before God, as was his custom. Notice that Daniel thanked God in the midst of his storm and fiery trial.

Praying and talking to God was more important than ever, and so he did not change his routine. What a feeling of peace he seemed to have despite the ordeal he was about to face.

It is amazing how king Darius, a non-believer, was able to recognise the power of Almighty God to save and keep Daniel. He says, 'Your God, whom you serve continually, He will deliver you' (Chapter 6:16). Darius knew Daniel's God would be sufficiently interested, loving, caring, available and aware of what Daniel was going through at that specific time in his life and would deliver him. How visible the presence of God must have been in Daniel's life. After all those years and trials, Daniel was still firm in his belief in God. His faith and confidence in God had not deteriorated over time but rather had increased with each trial. Daniel was completely assured of, and had every confidence in, the sovereignty of God in his life. Even when Nebuchadnezzar gave the command for all the wise men of Babylon to be destroyed, Daniel boldly and confidently went to the king, asking him for time so that he could tell the king the interpretation. After informing Shadrach, Meshach and Abed-Nego and them all praying together, God showed Daniel what the dream was in a night vision. In his prayer of thanks in the morning, he says, 'He [God] reveals deep and secret things; He knows what is in the darkness, And light dwells with Him' (Chapter 2:22).

God blessed Daniel in so many ways. He served under four kings in the courts and councils of some of the greatest monarchs the world ever had. Josephus calls him 'one of the greatest of the prophets', and the angel Gabriel calls him 'greatly beloved'. His life was active, long and fulfilled, yet he is remembered more because he was put in the lion's den. Daniel should be remembered for more than that. He should be remembered and respected for his faith, belief and obedience to Almighty God during some of the most trialling of circumstances.

What a lesson and inspiration! Just as God spoke to Daniel and gave him direction and peace in the midst of his situation, He wants to speak to you too and reveal deep and secret things. But He requires that you wait on Him until He speaks rather than trying to work it all out on your own. The words God reveals to you in secret will be a light to your path. You will know what to do next, and it will enable you to take the next step boldly and confidently.

Consequences of not believing the promises

Hard as it can be to believe the promises of God and be obedient to His voice, there is also a warning that we should heed if we choose not to trust His word and believe He will do what He said He would. We need only look at the Israelites. They were promised 'a land flowing with milk and honey', and the Lord told Moses to send men to spy out the land which He was giving to the children of Israel. Ten of the twelve spies who were sent came back with a bad report which included their exaggerations about the land being evil and its inhabitants being giants. These ten spies were convinced they could not take the land even though God had already promised it to them and it was theirs for the taking. The Lord said to Moses, 'How long will these people reject Me? And how long will they not believe Me, with all the signs which I have performed among them?' (Numbers 14:11).

God did forgive the Israelites but not one of the ten spies who brought the bad report entered the promised land. The Israelites were spared, but their entrance to the promised land was delayed. They suffered by wandering in the wilderness for forty years. This was one year for each day 'According to the number of the days in which you spied out the land' [forty days] (Numbers 14:34).

Focusing on what you see regarding your circumstances and your prodigal child with the natural eye, and allowing disbelief to creep in, can be costly. If God has clearly spoken through His word, you must wait and hold on to that no matter how the situation looks from your perspective.

Waiting on the promises

The waiting room of fulfilment is difficult, but it has a vital purpose and role to play in your walk with God. However, waiting is not something that God makes you do, and then, in turn, you get whatever you want. The time spent waiting allows you to gain a new perspective. Its purpose is to produce patience, develop character, understanding, maturity and most importantly, help you learn and grow in God. The writer of

Returning to the promises of God

Hebrews says that God made a promise to Abraham and 'after he had patiently endured, he obtained the promise' (Chapter 6:15). Although the battle in your mind might be raging and your situation speaks to the contrary, keep making the decision to obey God's voice, trust in Him and believe His promises.

Storms and fiery trials are opportunities for real faith in God to be tested and proven. When there is no backup plan, no way out and you have nothing else to lean on, you need to have faith in God and His word. The lyrics in the song 'Oceans'[ii] talk about God calling us out upon the waters, the great unknown and this is exactly where you are when your prodigal child is in the far country. You need to put your faith and trust in God and, as the song says, rest in God's embrace, knowing that you are His and that His grace abounds in deep waters just as much as it does on the mountaintops. His hand will continue to guide you and He will not fail you. As you spend time in God's presence, allow Him to remove the borders around your trust, walk with Him wherever He calls you and go deeper with Him into the great unknown. Your faith will increase as you do.

Wouldn't it be great if we could see our storms and fiery trials as opportunities to draw closer to God rather than automatically defaulting to focus on our troubles, the disappointments, change of plans and the sadness that it brings? If we could see our circumstances from a higher perspective, we would use the storms differently and get God's intended benefit from them. When I was thinking about that higher perspective, my mind went to that great bird of prey—the eagle. There are over thirty references in the Bible to the eagle(s). Isaiah 40 has one of the most beautiful promises in the Bible and it refers to the eagle. It says:

'But those who wait on the Lord shall renew their strength; They shall mount up with wings like eagles, they shall run and not be weary, they shall walk and not faint' (vs. 31).

If we are to better understand what this scripture actually means, it is important to know a little bit about this magnificent bird. There are over sixty eagle species in the world. 'Eagles are wonderful flyers, able to soar high, glide vast distances and plunge at terrifying speed' (Unwin and Tipling, 2018, p. 15). The eagle can spot its prey from 3 km [2 miles] away and can dive at 240-320 km/h [150-200 mph] (Unwin, 2016, p. 46). The eagle uses the winds and 'updrafts' from hills and mountains to gain altitude, save energy and prepare them for long soaring flights to another place, particularly when they are migrating large distances either north or south.

'Waiting on the Lord' does not imply a wishful thinking mentality. It indicates a confident expectation, one of hope and trust in God, knowing that He will do what He said He will. Those who do wait on the Lord will find that He will not fail them; that is just not a possibility (Henry, 1992). Instead of viewing the storms and fiery trials as winds of adversity, we need to see them and the updrafts as being part of the preparation to take us to that higher level and new place with God.

The word 'mount' has multiple meanings, including 'to rise', 'to grow', 'to soar', and 'to increase'. As you 'mount up', there is a transformation and growing that takes place within you as a person—having faith in God and allowing Him to take you there being the key to it. Matthew Henry explains it as follows, 'they shall mount up so strongly, so swiftly, so high and heaven-ward.... they shall press forward.... They shall walk, they shall run, the way of God's commandments.... with perseverance and therefore in due season, they shall reap' (1992, p. 1152).

Trials and tribulations can be mentally, physically and emotionally draining. But if you put your trust in God, your strength will be renewed and you will be able to labour, wrestle, resist and bear (Henry, 1992). The storms of life and the fiery trials will then be the very things that take you higher in your walk with God rather than blow you off course. 'Mounting up' should not be considered as stepping off the edge of a cliff unsupported. Exodus 19 says, 'You have seen what I did.... how I bore you on eagle's wings and brought you to Myself.... if you will indeed obey My voice and keep My covenant, then you shall be a special treasure to Me above all people; for all the earth is Mine' (vs. 4-5).

God has a plan for your life and that has not changed. The problem is we have become too comfortable and just 'as an eagle stirs up [arouses, provokes] its nest, hovers over its young, spreading out its wings, taking them up, carrying [lifting] them on its wings', so the Lord does the same to us (Deuteronomy 32:11). When that stirring begins, we must learn to move on with God rather than trying to dig our heels in and stay where we are.

Another problem we have is that we see our afflictions as obstacles that need to be dealt with immediately and removed rather than endured. We also tend to see our afflictions as permanent rather than temporal. Psalm 30 tells us that 'If weeping endureth for a night and it be a wearisome night, yet as sure as the light of the morning returns after the darkness of the night, so sure will joy [a shout of joy] and comfort return in a short time [in the morning], in due time to the people of God' (Henry, 1992, p. 782). Every affliction and storm we encounter will bring a new revelation of Jesus. Knowing and continually reassuring ourselves of the temporal nature of our afflictions will help lift our eyes so that we can start seeing the situation from that higher perspective rather than through the lens of disappointment. Holding on to the promises and learning to soar by mounting up on the word of God will sustain us through it and help bring that new revelation. Remember, you are a victor, not a victim of your circumstances. Yes, the way God moves may be different from how or when you expect, but one thing that you can be assured of is that it will be 'exceedingly abundantly above all that we ask or think' (Ephesians 3:20). Waiting on God, although not always our strong point, is vital. With your eyes fixed firmly on God, you are more than a conqueror over the things that would seek to imply otherwise, withhold your progress, and cause you to sink.

There is a time coming when you will look back on the way that the Lord has led you and be amazed at His mercy and goodness directing each and every one of your steps. The things you called adversities and evildoings were really blessings that moved you on in God. You will also see that your storms and fiery trials did not continue or last any longer than they should have. Each and every one of them is connected with the other and has all worked together for your good. You can 'count it all joy when you fall into various trials, knowing that the testing of your faith produces patience' (James 1:2-3).

Finding hope in the promises

As mentioned above, 3023 people, including Daniel and his friends, were captured during the siege of Jerusalem. Besides that, king Nebuchadnezzar destroyed the temple, the palace, the homes of the people and the city wall a few weeks afterward. Everyone was affected—the young, the old, male and female, the godly and the ungodly. It was a national tragedy. God's city had fallen into the hands of the Babylonians.

The prophet Jeremiah was in Jerusalem at that time, but he was not amongst those captured. He was heartbroken about this tragedy, which had unfolded before his very eyes, and he expressed his grief in the book of Lamentations. In his own words, he says, 'My eyes fail because of tears. My spirit is deeply disturbed; My heart is poured out on the earth [in grief], Because of the destruction of the daughter of my people [Jerusalem]' (Lamentations 2:11, AMP). Jeremiah was at a loss to find words to console the grieving women as they looked helplessly at their babies, who were dying of hunger. The whole sequence of events made him feel hedged into a confined space with no means of escape, a place where he, and others, would be left to die.

Throughout Lamentations, Jeremiah tries to help people face the pain they were experiencing rather than try to explain it away. In his own attempts to do so, he tries to change how he is feeling by recalling past experiences. However, remembering the past only made him feel worse—as though his soul was sinking within him. If we observe the five poetic chapters in Lamentations, we can see how Jeremiah moves from mourning to praising and then from praising to prayer for the restoration of the Israelites who had rejected God. The real turning point only came for Jeremiah as he started to remember the faithfulness, compassion and mercies of God. He remembered and proclaimed again that 'The Lord is good to those who wait for Him, to the soul who seeks Him. It is good that one should hope and wait quietly for the salvation of the Lord' (Lamentations 3:25-26). By focusing on your situation and problems, it will be harder to see a way out of them and you can become convinced that the situation is hopeless. The lesson that Jeremiah learned was that the key to moving forward was to focus on the faithfulness of God.

In Lamentations, this small book of five chapters, Jeremiah provides words of comfort and companionship for those who are suffering. Although he reflects on the purposes and results of suffering, Jeremiah does not forget to plant seeds of hope for the future rebuilding and restoration process. You, too, can find comfort and hope in the promises of God during your storms and fiery trials. No matter what comes your way, God remains faithful. There are, however, conditions to receiving God's promises and understanding divine things. These start with receiving the word(s) that God has spoken:

'My son, if thou wilt receive my words, and hide my commandments with thee; So that thou incline thine ear unto wisdom, and apply thine heart to understanding; Yea, if thou criest after knowledge, and liftest up thy voice for understanding; If thou seekest her as silver, and searchest for her as for hid treasures; Then shalt thou understand the fear of the Lord, and find the knowledge of God. For the Lord giveth wisdom: out of His mouth cometh knowledge and understanding' (Proverbs 2:1-6, KJV).

Having hope and faith in God will help you hold on to the promises so that you can trust with confidence and rest securely in them. It will also give you the courage and strength to keep going and overcome every storm and fiery trial that comes your way. Losing that hope will make you feel paralysed by your situation. Stay focused on God and proclaim as the Psalmist David did, 'For You are my hope; O Lord God, You are my trust and the source of my confidence from my youth' (Chapter 71:5, AMP).

As a child of God, you are in a covenant relationship with Him and should live by trusting in His promises even when everything seems to testify to the contrary. 'God never breaks or changes His promises. They are everlasting promises to which God committed Himself forever' (Sproul, 2018, p. 9). There is hope for you in the promises of God.

Power of the promise

As we come to the end of this first chapter, I want you to know without a doubt in your heart that there is power in the promises of God. There are so many accounts and stories from people in the past and present who could testify to this and that I could have drawn on. However, I have chosen one from the past for a number of reasons. Firstly, because it is about a mother and her prodigal child. Secondly, not only has it blessed and encouraged me, it is ending with resounding results, is known and speaks for itself. I trust this will bless you too and settle your heart as we prepare to move on to Chapter 2 and to hear the voice of God.

So many people across the world have sung or heard the renowned hymn 'Amazing Grace', but few may be aware of the story behind its author. John Newton's autobiography, edited by Vasile Lazar, says he 'was born as it were in His [God's] house and dedicated to Him' in infancy (Lazar, 2017, p. 15). John's mother taught him English at the age of three and at the age of four, he could read any common book put before him. In his own words, John says, 'she stored my memory, which was then very retentive, with many valuable pieces, chapters, and portions of scripture, catechisms, hymns and poems' (Lazar, 2017, p. 15). John was as willing to learn at that young age as his mother was to teach him.

There is no doubt that John's mother played a significant role in his early years, not just in his education but in lifting him up 'through many prayers and tears to God' (Lazar, 2017, p. 16). She raised him 'with a view to the ministry if the Lord should so incline' his heart (Lazar, 2017, p. 16). Sadly, John's mother died two weeks before his seventh birthday.

At the age of eleven, John's father, who was a commander in the Mediterranean trade, took him to sea. Throughout his teenage years, John turned against and rejected the Christian teachings. Despite spending his early adult years in 'riotous living', John was often disturbed and pierced with sharp convictions. Through the course of time, John 'sinned away all the advantages' of the early impressions his mother had on him.

A young man with such a fantastic beginning in the things of God who then walked away so far in the opposite direction of them. It took a ferocious storm and maritime disaster in 1749 to bring John to his

Returning to the promises of God

senses and change the course of his life. He began to know that there is a God who hears and answers prayers. Who would have thought that God would use a storm in the ocean to stop a prodigal like Newton in his tracks? Yet God chose this man with such a colourful past to pen the words of so many beautiful hymns, including 'Amazing Grace' (1779).

Once the Lord opened his spiritual eyes, John describes finding 'a great benefit from the recollection' of the things his mother had taught him (Lazar, 2017, p. 16). There is no doubt in John's mind that he also reaped the fruits of his mother's prayers and the things she taught him about the scriptures.

So many songwriters and authors, including Newton, have written about the transformational change that God has undertaken in their life, the goodness of God and the promises of God. Even though God himself has promised to work all things together for our good and to be with us in the storm, we still seem to find it hard to grasp and hold onto the promises of God. In one of John Newton's letters to his friend Thomas Haweis in 1763, he writes:

> *'Though all believers are tried at times—yet some pass through the voyage of life much more smoothly than others. But he 'who walks upon the wings of the wind, and measures the waters in the hollow of His hand' [Psalm 104:3] will not allow any of whom He has taken charge, to perish in the storms—though, for a season, perhaps, many of them are ready to give up all hopes'* (Lazar, 2017, p. 72).

As parents, we should be encouraged that our prayers and the things we teach our children about the scriptures and the ways of God are not in vain. God will bring them to the attention of the prodigal child as and when the time is right. There is nothing that God cannot use to turn things around for His glory. Part of our problem is that we are limited in our thinking about how He will fulfil what He has said He will do and indeed that He will actually do it.

Be encouraged; there is power in the promises of God. We serve a God who keeps His promises, who does not lie, is reliable, trustworthy and faithful to His word. John Newton wrote about it himself in the hymn Amazing Grace, 'The Lord has promised good to me, His word my hope secures. He will my shield and portion be, as long as life endures'.

John wanted his life to inspire others, and he asked God to 'give a history to all who may read these records [his lifetime of diaries] of thy goodness and my own vileness'.[2]

We need to play and continue to play our part as parents to faithfully inform and teach our children the scriptures and the things of God. The road and journey that God takes or allows them to go on thereafter are at His command and His doing. Continue to hold fast to the profession of your faith and embrace the gospel without wavering.

There is power in the promises of God. He will not allow His word to return unto Him void. We can see that in John Newton's account over two hundred years ago and it is still the same in testimonies today.

> *'There is strength within the sorrow, there is beauty in our tears, And you meet us in our mourning, With a love that casts out fear. You are working in our waiting. You're sanctifying us, When beyond our understanding, You're teaching us to trust.... You're with us in the fire and the flood. You're faithful forever.... You surround and you uphold me, And Your promises are my delight. Even what the enemy means for evil, You turn it for our good.... Even in the valley, you are faithful. You're working for our good, You're working for our good and for your glory'.*[iii]

It is time to return to the promises of God.

---

2. https://www.themorgan.org/exhibitions/online/TheDiary/John-Newton

Chapter 2

Hearing the voice of God

'Your ears shall hear a word behind you, saying 'This is the way, walk in it'. Whenever you turn to the right hand or whenever you turn to the left'.

(Isaiah 30:21)

My Early Childhood

Growing up in the countryside in Northern Ireland had many benefits, not least the opportunities to be loud or quiet, to think, be creative, explore and most importantly, to imagine and dream.

My dad was a builder to trade and a very hard worker. After doing his 'day job', he would come home and continue working until midnight to try and finish the home he was building for us. My mum was very proud of what he achieved, and she absolutely loved the home he built for her and us. Mum worked nightshift as a nurse in a local hospital and then slept while we were at school. She is such a character, full of fun, love and laughter. Stories of the things she and her friends used to get up to never cease to make us smile and laugh. Mum managed to fit a lot into her day and as much as she was happy and settled at home, she also loved taking us to the beach, out for picnics or into town.

The ground our home sat on and the surrounding fields were a huge adventure playground. Being the youngest child had its advantages and disadvantages. The seven-year and three-year age difference between us meant that the adventures of my siblings were more exciting to be part of—an advantage for me, of course. My attempts at reshaping their LEGO creations or ideas for adventures were not as advanced nor indeed welcomed—an obvious disadvantage for them! Climbing trees, playing tennis in the backyard, making bows and arrows, roaming through the fields [taking care to avoid the cows and the bulls], making daisy chains, playing on the haystacks, running errands to the shop, getting milk from the local farmer and helping my dad mix cement or concrete were just a few of our many adventures.

Early memories of the small rural primary school I attended are less positive than what they should have been or, indeed what I expected them to be. Negotiating a couple of miles along a busy main road on foot, with no footpath, in all sorts of weather seemed a huge and unfair ask from my perspective. Needless to say, we were not the only ones who had to walk to and from school. What made it more bearable were the days mum would bring us home for lunch. Opening the door to the smell of freshly baked griddle scones, soda farls, or wheaten bread made it all seem worth it.

As was the custom for many families, we attended church each week. Mum sang in the church choir for many years, and my sister and I were part of the church trampoline club for a while. Church was a few miles away, and so we all piled into my dad's car, dressed in our Sunday best and headed off. I recall the service being very somber and strict. Once you were seated, moving of any sort or even turning your head was a definite no-no! The wooden seats were hard and uncomfortable no matter which way you sat. We were allowed to take a toy with us to church but trying to narrow the choice down to one and leave the others behind was a hard decision to make each week. In the end, the effort and decision-making process was a pointless exercise because when we got there, we could not play with it for fear of making a noise and having everyone staring at us!

As well as attending church, my siblings and myself were sent to a local Sunday School, which, thankfully, was within close walking distance. Hearing stories from the Bible and learning scripture verses was extremely appealing to me. I could not get enough of it and I remember being really annoyed with myself if I could not remember the verses or stories. My Sunday School teacher gave me a small Bible one year for good attendance at the yearly prizegiving. I remember looking at all the lovely colourful pictures and would wonder how I would ever read it or indeed remember it all. Deep inside, I desperately wanted to hear and learn about everything that was in it. Regardless of my love and passion for Bible stories, my enjoyment at Sunday School was always dampened by having to colour in pictures at the end. Sorry to say, I never warmed to that activity!

One of the things I will never forget about my childhood is a poster which my mum and dad had on the wall at home called 'The Broad and Narrow Way'. It was based on the words of Jesus to His disciples in Matthew 7:13-14. Mum would tell me the story behind it and what it meant. Any time I walked past it, I would stop to look at it and would silently think to myself that I did not want to go on the broad road because that leads to destruction.

As the three of us got older, we started to find the church services dull and boring. After several weeks of trying to sleep in, to avoid going to church, my parents sat us all down together and asked why we did not want to go. The three of us responded that we wanted to go to church where people sang, clapped their hands and were happy. Looking back, it must have been quite a hard thing for my parents to hear, but it led them to start looking for such a church. As children, we had no idea what we were asking for or why we were asking but within each one of us, there was a longing for more of God. He used three children to confirm to our parents that God was calling us as a family into a deeper place with Him and it was time to take that next step into what He had for us. Looking back now, it was a big decision that my parents made to move away from a traditional church that they had been part of for a long time and step into something new and unknown. What probably made it even more difficult was that the decision to move did not come with the local Minister's approval.

At our new church, people sang or gave their testimony. We all looked forward to going every week to the services. One of the very first songs I remember hearing was called 'Live for Jesus'.[iv] It was sung by the Pastor's daughter, and the words have stayed with me throughout the years.

'Well, I want to be remembered
As the girl who sang her songs for Jesus Christ
Who was willing to lay down her life
And do His will no matter what the price

Well, I'm singing for the deaf man
Who can hear about salvation through my song
And I'm singing for the blind man
Who can see the light in me and come along

Chorus

Live for Jesus; that's what matters
And when other houses crumble, mine is strong
Live for Jesus; that's what matters
That you see the light in me and come along

There are times when I am tempted
To turn off this rugged road, I travel on
There are times when I say, 'Jesus
Can't You find another girl to sing Your song?'

Well, I know it's not that I'm the only one
Who can sing this melody
But He's chosen me to bless Him
And to lead me into what is best for me'.

Lyrics in songs have greatly influenced my life and walk with God as far back as I can remember. From the very first time I heard the song

'Live for Jesus', it has never ceased to challenge me about laying down my dreams and ambitions and living for Him no matter what the cost. It also constrains me to think about two questions, 'What will I be remembered for?' and 'What legacy am I leaving behind?'. This world has so many pleasures and opportunities to offer but at the end of the day, living for Jesus is the only thing that really does matter and which counts. Times are and can be so hard that it is tempting and possibly easier to turn away from it all and let someone else do the work for Jesus. But for some reason, God chose me for a particular purpose, and He continues to lead me into what is best for me. I trust and pray that others will see God's light shining and radiating through me and will come to know my Saviour for themselves.

Dreaming and imagining were two of my favourite childhood pastimes. Like most children, I tried to imagine what I would become in life, where I would travel, what adventures I would get up to, who I would marry and how many children I would have. Little did I know where life would indeed take me. Neither did I foresee that committing my life to Jesus at the very young age of four and a half would be the best decision I ever made. The friend I found in Jesus that day has never left me nor forsaken me. This has been and continues to be the journey of a lifetime, even with the mountaintop and valley experiences.

New adventures

I am grateful for Godly parents and for the many others who have influenced my life at different ages and stages. One book that my parents gave me as a fairly young child was called 'Little Pilgrim's Progress' (1952). This simplified children's version of John Bunyan's 'Pilgrim's Progress' is an adventure story of a Christian's journey through life. As a child, this little book, with its two hundred and fifty-six pages and small print, felt like a reading marathon to me. Even though I did not fully understand every word in the book, or its meaning at the time, it has had a profound and lasting impact on my life.

It was also at this same time that my family decided, after much prayer, fasting, and waiting on God, to move from Northern Ireland to Scotland. Moving somewhere far away was like a dream come true, a place for new adventures and opportunities. Going to a new primary school was definitely a major bonus and would have been a good selling point had that been part of the decision-making process! The reality of what it meant for my parents to leave my brother [who was starting a higher education course] and family members behind, and walk into the unknown, never crossed my mind.

Hearing and recognising the voice of God

Moving to Scotland presented the challenge of finding another lively church. After some searching and God's leading, we finally found what we were looking for. The congregation came from a wide geographical area and so midweek meetings took place in the form of house groups. My sister and I used to go to the house groups with my parents. One particular Wednesday night, for some reason, it was just my mum and me who had gone to the meeting. As we journeyed home, we were talking about being filled with the Holy Spirit. I had heard about being filled with the Holy Spirit and I desperately wanted that closer walk with God. So, when the car stopped, my mum prayed with me that the Lord would fill me with His Holy Spirit. He did, and at the age of eleven, for the first time, I heard that still small voice of God whisper in my ear.

It would take too long to share the numerous stories about the situations and circumstances God used throughout my life to draw me closer to Him and how He helped me to hear and recognise that still small voice more clearly. One of my favourite promises about the voice of God says, 'Your ears shall hear a word behind you saying 'This is the way, walk in it'. Whenever you turn to the right hand or whenever you turn to the left' (Isaiah 30:21). There have been so many times when I genuinely did not know which way to turn or which path to take. During those times, I have quoted this scripture back to God and asked Him to tell me what He wanted me to do. He has never let me down.

Hearing the voice of God

Hearing the voice of God and understanding the path He wants you to travel on can take many different formats. When multiple opportunities and choices have presented themselves, and all seem possible and attractive options, God has shown me the way forward by shutting doors and closing down the options he does not want me to take. The path ahead then suddenly becomes clear, and it is as though He silently says, 'This is the way; walk in it'.

It is one thing to hear the voice of God through various sources such as Pastors, daily reading guides, and online services. Knowing for certain and trusting that it is definitely God's voice that is speaking to you and not a personal desire or thought is something that takes time to develop. Asking and waiting for God to confirm His word through different means or sources is so vitally important.

Hearing the voice of God may be new to many people, but God has been speaking to mankind since He first created them. Genesis 1 tells us that 'God created man in His own image; in the image of God He created him; male and female He created them. Then God blessed them, and God said to them, 'Be fruitful and multiply; fill the earth and subdue it, have dominion over the fish of the sea, over the birds of the air, and over every living thing that moves on the earth" (vs. 27-28). Mankind was made to hear the voice of God; it is not a new concept. God called to Adam, and he replied, saying, 'I heard Your voice in the garden' (Genesis 3:10). He also spoke to Eve and she too heard the voice of God and replied.

Adam and Eve are not the only two people in the Bible that God spoke to. In fact, it is fascinating to think about the relationship that God had with others such as Noah, Job, Abraham, Moses, Elijah, David, and Samuel and the particular way in which He spoke to them all. Reading their life stories and accounts of what happened, they had what we recognise as 'conversations' with God. Let's take Noah, for example. God talked to Noah about the wickedness of the people. He shared His plans with him and told him why He was going to destroy the people on the earth at that time. He then gave Noah specific instructions on how to build an ark that would protect him and his family and told him which animals and what food to take in. It was not a one-off conversation; it was an ongoing dialogue throughout his life.

Similarly, with Moses, the intricate details God gave him regarding so many things, including the ten commandments; the laws concerning violence, animal control, property, the sabbath; moral and ceremonial principles; and justice. Let us not forget the phenomenal descriptive instructions which He gave Moses for the construction of the Ark of the Covenant; the table for the showbread; the making and care of the golden lampstand; the tabernacle and the court of the tabernacle; the garments for the priesthood and other priestly robes.

God did not only speak to characters in the Bible about building and constructing things. He gave them step-by-step instructions, and travel directions, and explained the arrangements and provisions He had made for food, water and accommodation. We can see that in His conversation with Elijah when He said, 'turn eastward and hide by the Brook Cherith, which flows into the Jordan. And it will be that you shall drink from the brook, and I have commanded the ravens to feed you there' (1 Kings 17:3-4). Later on, He then told Elijah to 'go to Zarephath, which belongs to Sidon and dwell there. See, I have commanded a widow there to provide for you' (1 Kings 17:9).

Accounts in the Bible are endless about God speaking to and with His people. In some instances, the words were instructional, directional and one-way, but there are many other examples of two-way conversations and communications with God. On other occasions, such as 1 Samuel, it was not God who initiated the conversation. We read, 'David inquired of the Lord saying, 'Shall I go and attack these Philistines?' And the Lord said to David, 'Go and attack the Philistines and save Keilah'…. Then David inquired of the Lord once again. And the Lord answered him and said, 'Arise, go down to Keilah. For I will deliver the Philistines into your hand" (Chapter 23:2-4).

None of the characters above had the same written text or visual images we have today. Yet God guided each one and gave them instructions to lead them step-by-step. The guidance was clear, precise and definitive. Notice, they did not have to strive to hear it. Throughout the scriptures, the voice of the Lord is described as powerful; majestic;

it breaks the cedars, like the sound of many waters; and as the sound of roaring thunder.

In addition to the direct conversations with characters in the Bible, God also spoke through prophets and other somewhat unusual ways, including the burning bush and Balaam's donkey! God can speak to us in whatever way He chooses, just as He says in His word, 'For God may speak in one way, or in another, yet man does not perceive it. In a dream, in a vision of the night, when deep sleep falls upon men, while slumbering on their beds, then He opens the ears of men and seals their instruction' (Job 33:14-16). We should not only expect God to speak to us but we should also familiarize ourselves with the various ways in which He can and does speak. Lana Vawser (2017), in her book 'Desperately Deep', very helpfully lists the various ways the Lord can speak (p. 93).

1. He will always speak through His word. He will never contradict Himself.
2. He can speak in an audible voice as He did in 1 Samuel [3:4-11].
3. He speaks in an internal voice into our hearts and into our minds.
4. The Lord speaks through the world. The beauty of creation testifies to God Himself (Romans 1:20).
5. He speaks through visions and dreams (Numbers 12:6, Acts 22:17-18).
6. The Lord may also appear before us, as in Acts 9.
7. He can speak through impressions or through a knowing (Nehemiah 7:5).
8. He also speaks through signs, nudges, books, children, newspaper headlines, movie names, circumstances, and prophetic dramas, even through some people's lives.

There is nothing in the Bible to suggest that God has stopped speaking to mankind. Part of the problem we have today is that there are so many voices, sounds, and un/spoken languages in the world, 'none of them are without significance' [message or meaning] (1 Corinthians 14:10). Distinguishing between these other voices and that of God, irrespective of the method He uses, will help stabilise you whether you have a mountaintop or valley experience.

One of the ways we can distinguish the voice of God from others is by knowing that He rarely asks us to take a step in faith and obedience without first giving us a promise or instruction. We can see that from the way He instructed the characters mentioned above. If we pray and listen to His voice, follow the leading of the Holy Spirit, trust and obey Him, rest upon His word, and wait on His timing, He will not only lead us step-by-step, but He will position us ready for the future He has planned for us. It is about faith, taking God at His word, knowing we can rely upon it, and declaring that God will do what He has said He will. As you do, be assured that He is faithful to His word and has never lost a battle!

The voice of God in my storm and fiery trial

Hearing the voice of God speaking directly into our circumstances can open our eyes to the wider picture, and we can start to see things from His perspective. If we are blinded by our circumstances, fears, or pre-conceived ideas, doubts and anxieties can creep in and we can become afraid of what is happening in our lives and with our families. Feelings of powerlessness and hopelessness sap the energy and life right out of us, and it is not long before we get disheartened and discouraged. Rather than walk in the knowledge and confidence that God has everything in control, we limp along hour by hour and day by day, fearing the worst.

Our natural instinct is not to look to God in the midst of our storm and fiery trial. When we recognise that and consciously change our thought process, not only will we be amazed at what God reveals, we will sense His presence. Once that happens, we can be content in our situation, knowing He is there with us, that He is in control and that His power is limitless. As the Psalmist says, 'I would have lost heart unless I had believed that I would see the goodness of the Lord in the land of the living' (Psalm 27:13).

This is all part of an incredible plan and journey that God has for your life. He is a God who is all-powerful, all-knowing, and always present. A God who is gracious, righteous, keeps His promises and leads us one step at a time. Martin Luther King captured it so well when he said, 'You don't have to see the whole staircase, just take the first step'.[3]

Hearing the voice of God while my prodigal child has been in the far country has been a new and unusual experience for me. Others may have had a similar experience, but I am unaware of it. In the early days after my child left for the far country, I continued to read my Bible, search for answers and tried to hear what God was saying to me in it all. God did and has continued to speak to me through His word, but I felt I needed to hear other people's experiences. I went to the books in my bookcase and with a simple prayer and tears streaming down my face, I simply said, 'God, I desperately need to hear a word from you about my situation'. That was the start of what I can only call the Holy Spirit's sequential ordering of books and words directly from Him about my situation. How some of the books in my somewhat small and select bookcase came to be there, I have no idea.

It may seem a hard story to believe, but the first book I picked up spoke directly to me about my situation at that time. Thereafter each book, not all of which were in the bookcase, was a follow-on from where I had left off in the last one. Every book became like a stepping stone that led and spoke precisely to me about my situation at that very time. It was not just recently published books that God used to speak to me either. While some had recently been published, others were several years old. For example, I found out that my grandfather had written two books in the 1920s. Although I do not know how many copies were printed at the time, it would seem that there are not many around. The copy that one of my family members has is therefore very precious. When I finally managed to see the copy and opened it up for the first time, there on the inside of one of the front pages were written the words 'No trial, however great, warrants a human soul's desertion of its maker—God has never failed'. A grandfather I never had the pleasure of meeting was used by God to write two books in the 1920s. God allowed at least one copy

---

3. https://www.goodreads.com/quotes/199214-take-the-first-step-in-faith-you-don-t-have-to

of each of these books to survive and make its way back into our family to speak to me almost 100 years later. Why? To remind me that He has never failed and to encourage me to keep going and stay focused on Him.

Initially, it was hard not to question myself over whether I was searching for and picking up a certain type of book that would speak to my situation rather than God's leading and sequential ordering of books. I desperately wanted to ensure I was hearing directly from God and was not holding onto words and promises that were not appropriate to me in this particular situation. On reflection now, I can see that I gave myself way too much credit for even thinking I was that clever! Nonetheless, at the time, I was pursuing God and asking Him to speak to me in ways I had no direct control or influence over and/or through people who did not know me, or anything about my situation. He was gracious enough to respond to my asks, and in the summer of 2018, my husband, one of our children and myself had traveled to Boston in the USA. I like to go to church if I can whenever I am away, and unbeknown to me, the hotel we were staying in was right next door to Hillsongs Boston. Part of the message that Sunday morning was about speaking life even when you cannot see it, believing God when you do not feel it, and to 'not grow weary while doing good, for in due season we shall reap if we do not lose heart' (Galatians 6:9).

During the same trip, we went to stay in another part of Boston and although there was very little to do there other than go for long walks, there was a retail shopping outlet not too far away. My husband wanted to go to the bookshop, and so we set off and walked the relatively short distance up the road. Again, I was asking the Lord to speak to me that particular day and I believed, and still do, that God can speak anywhere through anything. On entering the shop, we both went our separate ways to browse round this non-Christian bookshop. God led me, in that massive bookstore, to an aisle where my eyes lit on Louis Giglio's book called 'Goliath Must Fall. Winning the battle against your giants' (2017). As I started to skim read through parts of the book, tears began to stream down my face. Here I was, in a foreign country, and God was still speaking loud and clear, this time through a Christian book in a non-Christian bookshop.

Later on that year, we went back to Northern Ireland to see family and attend a women's conference that I had wanted to go to for a few years but had not previously managed to. On the Sunday, we went to the Whitewell Metropolitan Tabernacle in Belfast, and Pastor McConnell, one of my favourite speakers, was preaching. The message that day was taken from Mark 3:1-6, where Jesus asked the man with the withered hand to do what seemed impossible to him [to stretch it out]. I had been telling the Lord how impossible and hard I felt my situation was and how I was just existing, going through the motions and routines of life like a robot. Pastor McConnell went on to say in his sermon that even though your situation seems impossible, keep praying, stay faithful even when you feel nothing, keep going through the motions, step out in faith, and Christ will give you your breakthrough.

Similar things happened the following year when I was in New York. This time we went to visit Times Square Church. Again, I desperately longed and needed to hear from God. Sure enough, the Assistant Pastor spoke, and once more, the message was directly relevant to where I was in my journey at that time.

On another occasion, an uncle who is well up in years, lives quite some distance away, and does not know anything about my situation phoned me out of the blue and said, 'I have a message from God for you. God is faithful. He will do what He said He would do'. Not sure I heard much more of the conversation that day. I was just so overwhelmed by the Holy Spirit's efforts to speak to me.

To complement all this, every online sermon I listened to had something in it that either confirmed a promise God had given me, or it related directly to my situation at that time. Content in each one was consistent and emphasized: the need to press in with God, the waiting time was key to moving to the next step; God was preparing me for what lay ahead; what God has promised will come to pass; trusting God's timing; knowing what time it is, and hearing what God is saying.

There are new places and heights in God that He wants to take us to, which we have not even begun to imagine. The way to them is often through the valley experiences and over rough terrain. It is a narrow way, and we could easily get lost or go off track if we do not walk step-by-step with God. Being afraid of making a wrong move or taking the wrong path could result in us not taking any steps at all. Finding the courage to take the first step involves fixing our eyes on Jesus, reaching out to take His hand, and asking God to lead us on the path He has for us. As you take that first step, the light will shine on the next one. 'You'll understand what it means to walk through the dark times of your life with the comfort of His presence as your only light' (Omartian, 2008, p. 12).

On another occasion, I was on the treadmill listening to a service online. After the praise and worship, the preacher made his way to the pulpit. Before he started preaching, he looked directly at the camera and said words to the effects of '…. for you on the treadmill; God has given me a word for you. God wants to speak to you'. The tears started rolling down my face, and it was as much as I could do to finish my run. Once again, the words spoke directly into my situation—about what God was doing in my life, where I was in His plan and purpose at that time, and words of encouragement to keep going and not give up because breakthrough was coming. Unbelievable accuracy is the only way I can sum it all up.

It is hard to fully describe all the various ways in which God has spoken to me while my child has been in the far country without sounding overly boastful and hyper-spiritual. I would not for a minute want anyone to think that was an image I was trying to portray. My only part in it is that I cried out to God and asked Him to speak to me. Over these last few years, I have been overwhelmed by the pinpoint accuracy, the methods He has used, the level of detail, and His desire to communicate with me.

The quote I mentioned above by Martin Luther King was a plaque sitting on a bookcase in a meeting room that I went to at work. God's timing for me to be in that room and see the quote was absolute perfection because I had been reading Stormie Omartian's book 'Just enough light for the step I'm on' (2008). God had been speaking to me about putting my hand in His and letting Him lead me one step at a time. He used that quote to reassure me that I did not need to see the whole staircase. I just needed to take the first step and keep trusting Him to reveal enough light for the next one.

Should you take nothing else from this chapter, know and be assured that God sees you where you are, and He can, and He does, want to speak to you. Do not stop yearning to know and draw closer to Him. He may or may not speak to you in the way you think He should or desire Him to, but do not give up (Vawser, 2017). You can be assured that He will speak in the way He so chooses. While it is great to hear a word from God through other people, but when you learn to listen and hear His voice for yourself, nothing could or will ever surpass that.

In her book 'The Prophetic Voice of God' (2018), Lana Vawser talks about God 'calibrating her heart'. Calibrate simply means to adjust, regulate, attune, rectify or bring into line. Lana describes God doing that calibration in her 'little by little through each whisper' and how that, in turn, activated her faith (p. 14). When you have heard from God direct about your situation, and He has confirmed it, you will be able to shrug off any doubts or fears the enemy would try to flood into your mind—especially when your situation does not appear to be changing or getting any better. Hearing from God really does change everything. No matter what negative thoughts permeate your head or what situation you find yourself in, a divine interruption calibrates your heart and thoughts and will bring peace in the midst of the storm or fiery trial (Vawser, 2018).

Learning to listen to the voice of God means you need to draw aside from the busyness of everyday life. Finding that special place where you can meet with God can take time and will be different for everyone. Whichever time and place you decide upon, remember the words God spoke to Moses, 'Behold, there is a place by me, and thou shalt stand upon a rock' (Exodus 33:21-23, KJV). It is incredible to think that we have an invitation to a place beside Almighty God where we can 'sit near Him and receive the revelation secrets of His promises' (Psalm 25:14, TPT). Once you are in that secret place, do not be in too much of a rush to get away and get on with the next thing on your to-do list. Make time to linger in the presence of God. Use it as a time and place to 'Arise, cry out in the night.... Pour out your heart like water before the face of the Lord. Lift your hands toward Him for the life of your young children' (Lamentations 2:19).

Authors use a variety of terms such as 'the pruning process', to describe what is happening in the midst of our personal storms and fiery trials. Attaching a label can be a helpful way to understand and come to terms with what is happening in your life. But it is not as important as knowing and being completely convinced that God's desire is to be closer to you during the time that your child is in the far country. It was never intended to feel like a time of abandonment, or that heaven is silent. God cares about you during this time just as much as He does when you are enjoying a mountaintop experience. Of course, the process, the preparation, the waiting time, the next steps, and the future that God has planned for you are all important. God is waiting for you to do what Moses did, which was to turn aside. Once you do, God will likewise speak to you.

Waiting on God and listening for His voice is not something that can be rushed. It can be even harder to hear that still small voice when you do come into His presence because the time is spent in floods of tears, crying out in pain and grief over what is happening to your child, your family, and life as you knew it. Breaking through the underlying questions about why this has been allowed to happen to you can be harder than you think but God is so patient. He wants to hear everything that is in your heart, including the painful thoughts and feelings. After you have brought them all to the feet of Jesus and left them there, it is time to wait and listen to what He has to say. Once you do, you will find yourself waiting on, longing for, and living by every word that comes from His mouth.

Lessons from Joseph on hearing the voice of God

It can be hard to accept a plan for your children and family which is different from the one you have been praying about for many years. Hearing God speaking directly into your situation helps you understand a bit more about what is going on and be assured that God is in control. In reality, though, you still have to walk through each step of that plan. There will be times when you feel you are the only person in the world who has to

Hearing the voice of God

accept and come to terms with an alternative divine plan which does not remotely reflect your own plans and dreams for your family.

Well, take courage. You are not the only person to be going through an abrupt interruption to your life's expectations! Joseph of Nazareth is one of those unsung heroes of the Bible. He can often be overshadowed not only by the other characters in the nativity but also by 'Joseph the dreamer' in the Old Testament. The Joseph we are talking about is only mentioned by name in twelve verses of scripture.

Within those twelve verses, the information we get is limited. He was engaged to Mary; then, he became the husband of Mary. His occupation, although stated as a 'carpenter', comes from the Greek word 'tekton', which means ar-tif-icer or skilled worker/craftsman. A person with such an occupation was skilled not just in wood but in working with stone, iron, and copper. Joseph of Nazareth was a master builder. We are told in scripture that an angel appeared to Joseph on three separate occasions in dreams. There are no recorded words or references in the Bible to Joseph ever speaking. I call him the quiet man of the New Testament but do not underestimate him. He was a man whose actions speak louder than words. Although the Bible does not tell us Joseph's story in any detail, if you dig deep, you begin to get a glimpse into his life.

Imagine living in Bible days, and you find out the person you love tells you she is having a baby and you are not the father. The law says you are within your rights to divorce her as she has been unfaithful to you. How do you control the overwhelming and paralyzing nature of such a situation? How do you deal with the sheer volume of thoughts and rollercoaster of emotions going on inside your head and heart?

While you are trying to process that information and decide on your best course of action, an angel appears to you in a dream with the message that you are to go ahead and marry the woman you are engaged to—yes, the same person who you believe has betrayed your trust. You awaken from your dream and start to consider all possibilities. Option 1—you go with your original plan, divorce her quietly, pick up the pieces of your broken heart and try to find someone else to spend the rest of your life with. Option 2—you try to decide whether the dream is real or not but at the back of your mind lies the knowledge that God has not spoken to his people since the prophecies of Malachi, and why would he break His four-hundred-year silence to speak to you? Option 3—you choose to obey the message in the dream.

Some things that happen to us in life can be a result of choices we have made, and there is no one else to blame other than ourselves. Dealing with situations that are not of our own making can be a bit harder. After finding out that Mary was pregnant, Joseph had a major decision to make. It was a decision that would affect both their lives and their future. Had Joseph been an impulsive young man in his decision-making, he would probably have already 'made a public example of Mary or put her away secretly', but we read in Matthew 1:20 that 'he thought about these things'. The Greek word for thought is 'pondered', which means contemplated, mulled over, meditated, weighed it up. In other words, everything was revolving or rotating around in Joseph's head. Pondering is something that both Joseph and Mary had in common. In Luke Chapter 2, after the shepherds had visited, we read that 'Mary kept all these things and pondered them in her heart' (vs. 19).

Through Joseph's dream, God suddenly steps into what must have seemed a devastating and overwhelming situation. Joseph's actions tell us he chose to embrace the will of God for his life, as revealed in the dream. He chose to let go of the control of his life, to follow the voice of God. He chose to marry Mary and to call the child Jesus rather than follow the custom of the day and name a son after a male relative. If you look closely at the words in the dream, there is enough information in this first dream to tell Joseph what his next step should be and what decision he should make in his dilemma.

Hindsight allows us to see that the love Joseph had for Mary was pure and genuine. Theirs was an amazing love story—a love so strong, that it commanded respect, honour and dignity in ongoing difficult and challenging circumstances. Their love for each other, along with their faith and trust in God, would continue to be tested throughout their lifetime together. We are guilty of reading over the nativity story and not fully considering what was going on for the characters involved. The first two years of marriage for Joseph and Mary must have brought a tremendous amount of physical and emotional stress. In those early months of

Hearing the voice of God

marriage, one of Joseph's first tasks was to ensure that Mary, who at that time was heavily pregnant, was taken safely from Nazareth to Bethlehem to register for the Census. Having successfully managed that, can you imagine how Joseph must have felt when he could not find a place to stay for the night—knowing that Mary is about to have her baby. Can you feel a little of the anxiety and stress that Joseph must have felt? He had tried everything humanly possible, but his efforts must have seemed hopeless in trying to find a quiet, safe, and private place for his wife to give birth.

Joseph had been obedient and followed not just the voice of God in the dream. He had been obedient to the law of the land at the time by going to register. God saw that, and again, at the right time, He stepped in and made a way when there seemed to be no way. What a sense of relief Joseph must have felt at being offered a stable. Yet his job was not finished in merely finding a place. How do you turn a stable with animals and tools into a place suitable for your wife to give birth to the Son of God? Yes, he was a carpenter, a master builder, and he had the skills, but time was not on his side because the baby was on its way. Neither was there an opportunity to create the perfect quiet and idyllic atmosphere, especially as the stable did not belong to him.

No one mentions the loneliness of the stable, the emotions, the fear, or the tears. The birth of a child is a time when having family and friends is needed for emotional support. If ever there was a time for Joseph to feel ill-equipped, unprepared, and alone, it was in the stable. He had every right to look at his circumstances and say, 'surely this cannot possibly be the will of God'. Yet the timing of it all was prophetic. If we could ask Joseph how he managed these difficult days and what helped him get through them, I believe he would say, 'It was the promises God gave me in the dream through the angel—She *will bring forth* a Son. You *shall call* His name Jesus. *He will save* His people from their sin. I believed that the words spoken were relevant to my situation, and I held on to them. Despite the dark times, I knew if I did my part, God would be faithful to His word and He would keep His promises'.

Time allows us to look back at the sequence of events that unfolded in Joseph and Mary's lives, but in those early days, I wonder what was going through their heads. Yes, the word and promises were clear. Look at the words spoken to Mary 'rejoice; you are highly favoured; the Lord is with you; you are blessed; do not be afraid; you have found favour with God; you will bring forth a Son—He will be great—He will be called the Son of the Highest; the Lord God will give Him the throne of His father David; He will reign over the house of Jacob forever, of His kingdom there will be no end; the Holy Spirit will come upon you; the power of the Highest will overshadow you; for with God nothing will be impossible'. But what exactly did this all mean? The arrival of this baby, may have initially seemed like an interruption to Joseph and Mary's lives, to the plan they had for their future, but after He arrived, did they think that life would settle down and they would carry on as a normal family?

Just when it seemed that might be the case, their lives and plans were once more interrupted by a visitation—this time by wise men from the East. Ever wonder how that conversation went? Maybe you think Joseph and Mary stood silent and watched as some wise men entered the house, fell down and worshipped the young child, handed over the frankincense, gold, and myrrh, then got up and left without saying a word. Maybe they did, but I think they would have had a conversation and shared their stories and experiences.

After they left, Joseph did not have much time to process the information and everything that had just happened, before the Lord appeared to him in another dream. It could be that prior to Jesus' birth, Joseph had no communion with God in such a manner as this. Now he has had not only one dream but two. This time, there is something different about the message—it carries a sense of urgency 'arise, take the young Child and His mother, flee to Egypt'. The word 'flee' in the Greek means to run away or to vanish. How do you tell your wife in the middle of the night, 'honey, we need to pack our things, we are going to Egypt, and we need to leave now!'

Prior to this dream, Joseph was not aware of the danger that the young child was in nor his need to escape it. It is the middle of the night. Joseph is tired after a long day, but he must make a decision again on whether to follow the voice of God. The trials and tribulations this young couple faced must have seemed relentless at times. I wonder what was

Hearing the voice of God

going through Joseph's head as he was preparing to go. If it was you or I, we would most certainly have queried it—'Egypt... are you sure? Egypt is famous for idolatry, oppression, dictatorship, and hostility to the people of God. It is a house of bondage and particularly cruel to infants. The journey itself will be long, inconvenient, and perilous to us all. Egypt.... really?'

Joseph was not disobedient to the heavenly vision. He made no objection; rather, he was diligent in his obedience. He could have said, 'I will ponder over this dream and if it is still with me in the morning, we will set off bright and early'. Instead, he set off on that long journey with complete dependence upon God. I call it blind obedience to the voice of God—not blind in the physical sense but spiritually. He did not question the voice of God. If this had happened to us, we would have a number of questions. Namely, 'have I really heard from God? How long will I be there? What do you mean 'stay there until I bring you word?' A word from who? Where will we stay? How will I get a job and provide for my family?' Not Joseph; he is content with the instruction 'Flee to Egypt, and stay there until I bring you word' (Matthew 2:13).

Some commentators think it was some seven years until Herod died. Others think it was a matter of months. Regardless, Joseph and Mary were quite a distance from the temple and the service that brought with it. In Egypt, they would be in the midst of idolators, and they had every right to feel far away in a strange and foreign land. Although Egypt was only for a season, neither Joseph nor Mary was given a timescale as to when it would end. Yes, they may have been hiding in Egypt, but it was not God's intention to leave them there.

I have thought so much about Joseph—the man who heard from God through dreams, the man who spoke with shepherds, who talked with Simeon and Anna in the temple, the man who spoke to wise men from the East, the man who pondered things in his head and heart. I would love to ask Joseph 'What made you so impulsive on this occasion? What made you rise from that dream in the middle of the night, leave everything behind and set off for Egypt?' If he were here, I think he would say, 'I have learned to recognise the voice of God and discern the truth. I trusted the promises He gave me in the first dream, and He did not let me down. No matter how crazy this instruction seemed or how foolish I might look, I was willing to be obedient and take the risk'.

Joseph was open and receptive to hearing from God. He totally abandoned his own desires and chose God's will for his life. Joseph sacrificed his need for understanding. I believe God granted Joseph quietness in his soul and confidence in the midst of conflict and fear. Obedience is not always attractive but do not underestimate the power of walking with God in the wilderness, across a desert, through storms, or during your fiery trial. Blind obedience will help increase your faith in God with each step you take.

We know so little about Joseph other than some of the places he lived, the things he saw, and a little about what he thought or must have felt. Joseph must have had so many questions, such as, 'God, why did you pick me to be your Son's earthly father?' Raising a child is a challenging prospect at the best of times, but how do you raise God's son? Yes, Joseph had a great honour placed upon him not only to be the husband of the woman who would carry God's son but to love, care for and help to raise this wonderful Child. The task placed on Joseph came at a price, yet it is mingled with honour, privilege, and blessing to be chosen for such a role. Being specifically chosen by God and given promises did not make him exempt from trials and tribulations. It was a time to hold onto the promises that God had given him and not to be afraid. Joseph had to learn to trust God. Neither did it mean that Mary and him would not at times feel afraid and overwhelmed. But the promise from God was clear. He said He would take them through. It is always easier to look back and see what God has done in your life than it is to look ahead and see what He is going to do.

Joseph had nothing this world today would want or possibly even admire. Yet, throughout eternity he will be known as a man of honour, faith, mercy, humility, and service. God chose Joseph because he had a heart that He could use, and he was willing to obey the voice of God. These are qualities that constitute greatness in the sight of God. Look at Joseph's journey. He was a man to whom God revealed the secrets of heaven. Joseph was the man who would teach and pass on the skills of his trade to the young child Jesus. Yes, it was hard, and it most definitely was an interruption to his plans, but I do not think Joseph would have swapped a minute of it. Each time God spoke, Joseph listened and faithfully obeyed. He was a simple man who played a key role, and he did so with great courage and honour.

Do not ever doubt God's power and desire to work in and through your life to accomplish what He has planned for you. 'He will achieve infinitely more than your greatest request, your most unbelievable dream, and exceed your wildest imagination' (Ephesians 3:20, TPT).

His love still amazes me and if you let Him, He will amaze you too.

Chapter 3

Friends

'Thou wilt keep him in perfect peace, whose mind is stayed on Thee because he trusteth in Thee. Trust ye in the Lord forever, for in the Lord Jehovah is everlasting strength'.

(Isaiah 26:3-4, KJV)

Friendship groups are something that parents have a measure of control over when their child is young. As they get older and start to form new friendship groups, parents no longer have that same influence over who their child spends time with. Regardless of age, most parents want to be assured that the people who come into their child's life and with whom they develop close friendships will be dependable, trustworthy, a good influence, loyal, caring and, of course, share the same positive values and morals. Having Christian friends does not always guarantee any of those things. In fact, some non-Christian friends can often appear to be more supportive, loyal, and, at times, the better friend! Maintaining the right Christian attitude towards your prodigal child's friends, can sometimes be nothing short of challenging. Rightly or wrongly, we make connections between the negative changes we see in our children and their friendship group. The right approach is, of course, to pray for them, but prayers can ricochet between asking the Lord to bless and save them, and then asking Him to keep them away from your child.

Making comparisons against your own experiences of friendships, and indeed, your values, expectations, and beliefs is only natural. Nonetheless, changing the way you think and feel about your child's friendship group is challenging—especially if you consider them to be negatively influencing your child and having played a part in leading them into the far country. Through frustration, annoyance, and a sense of justice, some of your child's friendship group may not, in your opinion, deserve the forgiveness of a loving, merciful Saviour! Finding forgiveness in your heart and loving them the way Jesus would want you to can be really difficult.

Finding forgiveness

Jonah in the Bible is a prime example of someone who did not want God to be merciful to others, namely the people of Nineveh. We have so much to learn from his experience and attitude towards others who, in his opinion, did not deserve to be forgiven. Alexander White (1952), in his book 'Bible Characters, calls Jonah the 'elder son' and the 'unmerciful servant of the Old Testament' (p. 381). Jonah has also been described as the 'reluctant missionary' and the 'only case in the record of scripture where a true prophet of the Lord tried hard to thwart the will of God by fleeing from the task that God had given him' (Nelson, 2018, p. 1318). What a reputation!

What makes the story of Jonah more amusing is the fact that the people of Israel 'were not a maritime people, but rather [they] had a great fear of the sea' (Nelson, 2018, p. 1318). Nonetheless, Jonah's fear of the sea was not as powerful as his repulsion to the idea that the people of Nineveh may escape the doom and destruction forewarned by God. Nineveh was approximately forty days away from being totally destroyed by God, and for a multitude of reasons, Jonah did not want to accept or submit to the divine will, plan, and purpose of God for His life. He thought if he could just escape until after the forty days, he would be off the hook, and the people would get the punishment they deserved. Jonah did everything he knew how to avoid obeying the instructions God had given him. At the root of it all, He did not want the people of Nineveh to hear the words of warning God wanted to tell them regarding their sinful ways. And he most definitely did not want their lives to be spared.

Jonah's story demonstrates the compassion and mercy Almighty God has and shows toward the wicked even when they do not, in our opinion, deserve it. He cares about others just as much as He cares about you and me. We are also challenged by Jonah's experiences of the need to avoid exalting ourselves over others. God loved and cared about the Ninevites so much that He saved them and spared their lives. He did not save them because they deserved it. He saved them because He loved them. Almighty God forgives, blesses, and is able to be gracious, kind, and patient with whomever he chooses. It is our thinking which needs to be reformed, and we need to see those, who we may not particularly like, or care for, through the eyes of Jesus.

After everything that Jonah went through—the mighty tempest on the sea, being thrown into the sea by the sailors, swallowed by a great fish, spending three days and three nights in the belly of the fish, and personally experiencing the mercy of God—you would think Jonah 'would now be the best prophet God ever had' (White, 1952, p. 384). Through it all, he still had to come to terms, not just with the divine will of God, but with the realisation that God was in control. The book of Jonah serves as a reminder to us about the sovereignty of God and His control over creation to fulfil His plans and purposes. We see how the Lord had prepared a great fish. He also prepared a plant and made it come up over Jonah to protect him from the sun. Then He prepared a worm to damage the plant and take it away again. After that, God sent a vehement east wind. God was in control and directed all of it.

Finally, we read that Jonah 'remembered the Lord and prayed' (Jonah 2:7). He reiterates his faith in the Lord, renews his commitment, and surrenders his will to the divine plan and purpose of God. 'But I will sacrifice to You with the voice of thanksgiving; I will pay what I have vowed. Salvation is of the Lord' (Chapter 2:9).

God was in control of everything in Jonah's life, and He is still in control of everything in your life and your child's. Your child's friends are not in control of their life. God is. Alexander White (1952) captures it so accurately when he says, 'Seas and skies and storms and fair weather all work together under the most complex and the most majestic laws for our good' (p. 384). Jonah could never have foreseen how God would use creation to put him back on track and position him for the task ahead. Likewise, it may be hard for you to see how everything is going to work out in God's great plan for you, but it will.

Finding forgiveness towards your prodigal child's friends can be challenging. Of course, we know the theory behind it and that if we do not forgive them, God will not forgive us. During my own experience, God allowed me to hear how a parent of one of my child's friends was feeling about their child and how they had 'gone off the rails'. Hearing their story, and feeling their heartache brought about a change in my own perspective and thinking. I started to see their whole family differently. My frustrations gradually turned into prayers for their whole family. I realised that if this situation was difficult for me and I have the Lord leading and guiding me and my family, how much more difficult must it be for parents who do not have the Lord and have no one and nowhere else to turn.

God is in control

Relinquishing control over your child is easier when you see them begin to mature into adulthood and move in the right direction for their future. This could be in terms of them gaining employment or going on to further/higher education. But it is also true in terms of seeing your child growing in the things of God and moving into the plans and purposes He has for their life. There is nothing more satisfying. In contrast, however, when a prodigal child heads off to the far country, it does not afford a parent the same opportunity or satisfaction to release them in the same way. Indeed, the opposite is the case, and you naturally want to hold them closer and tighter because you can see further down the road of destruction than they can and what could potentially lie ahead, should they continue in that direction.

I came across a book in my bookcase called 'The Lord is My Shepherd' by Clarence Sexton (2001). Where this secondhand book came from or how it got to be in my bookcase, I have no idea. Several words and paragraphs throughout the book had already been underlined. At the front, it also has the words 'A great book' and the date 20/06/03 written beside it. Although I am not an advocate of underlining or writing on books, I feel that I owe a huge thank you to whoever underlined it and wrote the comments on the various pages.

One day, in particular, things seemed to be getting worse all around me, and everything felt really foggy. Tears had become an ever-present constant companion, but they were suppressed until those times of the day or night when I could be alone with God, and then they would erupt like a river bursting its banks. In sheer desperation and longing for God to speak to me, I went to my bookcase and quietly prayed, 'God, I need to hear directly from You about my situation'. Randomly I reached out and pulled out the first book that came to me. As I began to open up the book and turn each page, the underlined text somehow seemed to be enlarged and illuminated before me. Not only that, they spoke directly into my situation at that specific time and season. Here is just one example:

> *'It looked to Samuel as if the kingdom were out of control. Saul's life was certainly out of control, but God was still in control. We seem to have the idea that when things around us are falling apart, the whole world must be coming apart at the seams as well. When we see families torn apart or experience difficulties in our own lives or in the life of the church that we are attending, we need to be reminded that God is still in control. He has never lost the reins... For us not to worry, we must realise that 'the Lord is at hand'.... We need not worry about anything because God is in control'* (p. 16-17).

As a parent and a mother, my heart was completely broken. I could not influence, change or control any of what was happening around me. Although we can accept, to some degree, that there are things we cannot change or control, being unable to positively influence and protect your child can be unbearable. This does not necessarily mean we are controlling or domineering, but as Christian parents, we know the far country is so evil, wicked, and perverse. Not only do its short-lived temptations look so appealing, but ungodly 'friends' are also overly eager, in their search for happiness and contentment, to explore the latest novelty and pleasure-seeking thrills, without realising the high price tag that comes with them. Many would argue that sin is pleasurable and maybe so, but it always pays out wages in due course.

I did not know where to even begin in trying to identify or define the turmoil, fears, and anxiety that was going on inside. Neither did I know what to pray for. There was a constant battle going on in my head over my role and responsibilities as a parent. I felt I should be sorting it out, positioning myself somehow, or changing things to alter the direction of travel, but I simply could not. The situation was so much bigger than me, and only God could sort it out. To surrender it all was somehow to have failed in my role and responsibilities as a parent. I could feel it slipping further and further out of my control, and I did not know what to do, or better still, what God wanted me to do.

It is during times such as these that God is faithful. Once again, He used Clarence's book to speak to me:

'We all have people and things that are difficult to give to God. You may believe that you cannot let go of your children. However, it is not that you cannot, it is that you will not. You may not trust your loved one to do the right thing; however, you must trust God to do the right thing with that person. Final surrender to God does not necessarily mean that God is going to move in a flash to do something, but it does mean that the moment we commit it to God, He will give us peace in knowing that He will take care of it' (2001, p. 17).

Clarence writes about the 'sweet peace' he found as he yielded his own life to God but also as he gave his children to the Lord, recognising they were a gift from Him. He tells about the comfort in realising that God is in control and He is always working even when we may not see it. It is we who condition our mind to believe that God is not doing great things. The ways in which God works means He will get the glory rather than us. As we look at our situations, we appreciate the words of Jesus afresh in Matthew 19, 'with men this is impossible, but with God all things are possible' (vs. 26). God makes a way when there is no way. As we realise that, our reliance on God increases and we come to the understanding that only God can turn our situations and chaos around. Only He can save a person.

Seeing how '*all* things work together for good to those who love God' is going to turn out, in reality, is hard, if not somewhat impossible (Romans 8:28). In fact, it simply does not look like *any* of it is going to work out for good. Rather, it seems as though destruction, hurt and pain are all that will become of it.

I have mentioned already that God has, for the most part of this season in my life, spoken to me through the sequential ordering of books. Well, on one occasion, He used a different way to show me what He meant by Romans 8:28. While working from home, I got that phone call which every parent dreads. One of our children called to say that they had an accident in their car. On hearing that kind of news, it is natural to go into automatic pilot and deal with the situation. Only afterward does the rush of emotions come flooding in, and you begin to think of the 'what ifs'. As I stood and looked at the mangled mess of the car, I had a fresh visual revelation of how much God had been and was still in control of everything in our family. He prevented the car accident from being much worse, even fatal. Our child walked away with nothing but a few scratches and bruises. The car, however, was a write-off. Not only did the situation seem bleak, but the way ahead also looked long and overshadowed by hurdles that would need to be overcome. To my surprise, God took this whole situation and literally turned it around overnight and brought something far better out of it than I could ever have imagined. He did it, and He did not need my help! A few days later, we went back to the scene of the crash to remove any personal belongings from the car. And as I stood there in the stillness of the aftermath, thinking about everything, I heard that still small voice whisper in my ear, 'I can bring something good out of something terrible'. At that moment, I was conscious of having just learned another lesson!

Focus on what God is doing

When a prodigal child is in the far country, some of the first things that are impacted and challenged is your friendship and relationship with them. From my perspective, conversations with my prodigal child felt strained. I felt tongue-tied and restricted to non-Christian topics instead of exchanging conversation on things God had blessed us with, an inspirational thought in a book, or things we were involved in at church. It also did not help relationships when the voice and opinions of 'friends' were more welcomed and adhered to than those of loving Christian parents and the many years of experience and wisdom! I could not understand or express how I felt inside. In my quiet times with God, it externally translated itself, like very deep, deep emotional sobbing, mostly without words, in a curled-up position on the floor at the side of my bed. Understanding and trying to make sense of those challenges and the emotions and feelings that go along with them, is really important.

Attachment theories are one way of helping us to understand a bit more about the strong emotional reactions that occur when affectional bonds are challenged, threatened or indeed broken. John Bowlby, a British psychologist, considered attachment and dependency in adulthood as different from childhood but he felt they remained active throughout a person's life (in Holmes, 1993). He also viewed the parental home as an important anchor point. Other sociologists (Allatt, 1996) believe that a happy, loving, caring relationship between a parent and a child is a secure emotional foundation from which a child can build for the future (in Brannen and O'Brien, 1996). These theories are great and have since been developed and expanded over the years. They do, however, primarily focus on the *child* and topics such as: how the early years of a child's life are important; adult attachments; multiple attachments, etc. Focus on the *parent* and attachment theory(ies) tend to look more at grief and loss.

During the early years of a child's life, there is a closeness between a parent and a child, which is hard to fully explain or define. It is a bond that can sense and know something is wrong without always being told or hearing any words spoken. For many, the attachment can be so deep that they can physically and emotionally feel the hurt and pain their child goes through even though the circumstances are not personally affecting them. While the relationship between a parent and a child is an individual thing, it is a timeless experience and lifelong (Rodgers, 1963: In Mearns and Thorne, 2007). It carries on through generations, and its success does not depend on things like material possessions (in Mearns and Thorne, 2007 and Durkin, 1995). The friendship between a parent and a child has formed over many years and developed from simple baby language to including them in family decision-making and adult conversations.

You may wonder why I have mentioned attachment theories in this book. Well, accurately defining and putting into words the emotions and feelings I was experiencing at this time has been difficult to capture. The only way I can personally describe my own reaction is one of grief and lament. I felt continuous attacks and attempts to sever the really close attachment and bond I have with my child. No day went by without deep, deep crying and calling unto the Lord. The pain and sorrow were so profound. Some days were hard to get through. Worry and anxiety would come in unexpected waves. Each time they did, I cried out more earnestly and poured out my heart to the Lord. Some books I read at the time talked about praising the Lord in the midst of the storm. Although I knew to do that, and did do it, my sorrow and seeming loss felt bottomless and hard to shake off. Re-reading and reminding myself of the promises God had given me was a lifeline. Not only did I find great comfort in holding on to those promises, but it also helped me focus on God, and what He was doing in it all, and reassured me that He had it all in control.

Throughout the many seasons of my life, when tumultuous thoughts and anxieties have tried to overwhelm me and steal my peace, I would quote Isaiah 26 over and over. 'Thou wilt keep him in perfect peace, whose mind is stayed on Thee because he trusteth in Thee. Trust ye in the Lord forever, for in the Lord Jehovah is everlasting strength' (vs. 3-4, KJV). It continues to bring comfort, which can only be compared to that which a child receives from a parent or family member when something has happened to them, or they are upset.

One day, again in desperation and wanting to hear from God, I lifted Clarence's book and there, on one of the pages, these words, taken from 1 Samuel 16:1 (KJV), were underlined. 'How long wilt thou mourn?'....

In so many words, how long are you going to be upset about this? How long will you live without trusting Me in this matter?' (2001, p. 17). It was a real wake-up call, and I felt the Lord saying that it was time to stop crying and dry my tears. Just like Samuel, I had to learn that God was in control of what was happening to my prodigal child. Although I knew it in my head, there needed to be deeper confidence in my heart. As I read through 1 Samuel 16, I could see how the Lord was at work in David's life as a young shepherd boy. Some of the preparation times that David went through would terrify us today as parents, especially when we read that he attacked and killed a lion and a bear after they took a sheep from the flock! No parent would ever want their child, no matter what age, to even attempt such a thing. David did not know what lay ahead for him, but God was in control and was preparing him for the plan that He had. This preparation would mean that David would fearlessly and confidently tackle Goliath, in the not-too-distant future. When he did, David would be fully prepared, equipped, and have the right mindset to do the job without fear or hesitation!

Friend of God

This chapter started by reflecting on children's friendship groups and finding forgiveness towards others. While I value the numerous people who have enriched my life in so many ways, the greatest friend I have ever had is the Lord Jesus himself. Amazingly this friendship offer has also been available to every generation that ever has or ever will come into existence. Joseph Medlicott Scriven, an Irish poet, captured it so beautifully in his hymn 'What a friend we have in Jesus'[v] (1855). Many of us will have sung this hymn numerous times, possibly without knowing the story behind it or where it originated.

Joseph Scriven came to know the Lord Jesus after losing his bride-to-be in a tragic drowning accident on the night before their wedding. In 1845 he decided to move to Canada to start a new life. Some ten years later, he received word that his mother was terribly ill, so he wrote her a poem called 'Pray without ceasing'. The words were penned sometime after

Scriven's own personal tragic loss of his bride-to-be. However, it could be argued they were also written 'from a Christian's desire to explain his own secret [tragic loss], with a view to helping someone else who was dear to him', namely his mother.[4]

Around 1857, Joseph Scriven fell in love again, but sadly, this time, his fiancée became ill and died of pneumonia. The poem was later retitled by Charles Crozat Converse, too, 'What a friend we have in Jesus' and then set to the music we are so familiar with today. The poem or hymn as we know it focuses on the friendship of Christ, and it is written in a 'question and answer' format.

Some of the topics for the questions centre around—being weak, heavily laden, our sins, sorrows, sighs, dis-peace, discomfort, and distress. The message of the hymn is simply that no matter what your question or problem is, the answer is the same, 'Take it to the Lord in prayer' because there you will find that intimate fellowship with Jesus, who is your friend.

Researching the stories behind some of the songs and hymns mentioned throughout this book has been a wonderfully uplifting experience. Sadly, some of these were written after times of great sorrow and loss. Yet even in the face of pain and tragedy, songwriters continue to show us how they found comfort in the arms and friendship of Jesus. They point others to the source of their unshakeable faith, joy and friendship, all of which they found in Jesus.

Never have I been more aware of the fact that God wants and has proven Himself to be a true friend to me. He has heard me every time I have called. The lyrics in the chorus of a song we sing in church simply say, 'I am a friend of God, He calls me friend'. It then goes on to say, 'Who am I that You are mindful of me, that You hear me when I call. Is it true that You are thinking of me, how You love me, it's amazing'.[vi] We are called to be friends of God and to have that fellowship or companionship with Him. Once you see the value in that, then it will become a more natural instinct to want to spend time with God and tell Him the

---

4. https://www.stempublishing.com/hymns/biographies/scriven.html
   http://www.biographi.ca/en/bio/scriven_joseph_medlicott_11E.html

thoughts, anxieties, fears, and desires in your heart, just as you would do with any genuine, physically close friend.

Times spent in God's presence, opening up and sharing your innermost thoughts, knowing He will never reject you for it, nor will He get tired listening to you, is so precious. Your storm or fiery trial is, therefore, something you may have to go through to get to the place or become the person God wants you to be. I am no one special that God should hear me when I call, but He has, and He will continue to. You need to know today that not only does God want to be your friend as well, but He also hears you each and every time you call.

I do not know what your story is. Maybe you have been let down by family or so-called friends and are afraid to trust again. Just by way of a reminder, friendships can form through sharing and discussing general information or having deep conversations. Others will form around similar interests or hobbies. Some friendships are formed quickly; others can take time to develop. Although there is no specific formula for developing friendships, there are some simple keys and principles which facilitate these multifaceted bonds. They include spending more time with that person and getting to know them better. Close relationships do not happen overnight; it takes time to get to know someone and feel comfortable in their presence. Time is a powerful ingredient to bond a friendship but also to use to talk together and listen to each other. Friendship grows as you begin to see the other person as someone who can be trusted and relied upon, someone you can open up to. Regardless of how long you have been a Christian, make time today to form that friendship with Jesus.

As we prepare to leave Chapter 3, I want you to know and be 'confident of this very thing, that He who has begun a good work in you will complete it until the day of Jesus Christ' (Philippians 1:6). Yes, it can be challenging to hold on to the promises of God during your fiery trial or when your emotions are so tossed about by the waves of the storm. Focusing on what seems to have been lost, rather than on what God is doing in and through your storm or fiery trial naturally comes so much easier somehow. Scripture urges us to take our eyes off our storms and fiery trials because when they become our focus, and not what God is doing in and through them, we can become stuck. Our natural eye tries to look ahead, and it cannot see how or when the storm or fiery trial will change or improve. Circumstances only appear to be deteriorating, and so the emotions and heartbreak take control over your focus. The fog which can linger about during your storms and fiery trials, therefore, does nothing but disorientate you, create blind spots, and cause confusion!

There are supernatural encounters waiting for you, but first and foremost, you need to look above your circumstances and disappointments. Remember, God is in control. Focus on what He is doing in and through it all. Most importantly, be assured that you are a Friend of God, and He loves you and your prodigal child.

Chapter 4

Unshakable faith

'In this, you greatly rejoice, though now for a little while, if need be, you have been grieved by various trials, that the genuineness of your faith, being much more precious than gold that perishes, though it is tested by fire, may be found to praise, honour and glory at the revelation of Jesus Christ'.

(1 Peter 1:6-7)

I remember one of our children saying to me one day, 'mum, you have unshakable faith in God'. Those words took me completely by surprise, but it got me thinking not just about why they said it but, more importantly, what does it mean to have 'unshakable faith'. Having given my heart to Jesus at such a young age, I have never known anything other than to put my trust in God but at no time had I claimed to have 'unshakable faith'. The word 'unshakable' means steadfast, resolute [firm], constant [relentless], unwavering [solid], entrenched [rooted], immovable, unflinching [persistent], unswerving [unshakeable], sure [unquestionable], firm [secure]. 'Faith' means confidence, trust, reliance, conviction, belief, assurance, devotion, loyalty, constancy, and allegiance. Who would have thought that the phrase 'unshakable faith' was so 'loaded' in its interpretation and meaning?

Many of us will have heard and indeed have quoted another common phrase, 'everything that can be shaken will be shaken'. This phrase is a derivation from Hebrews 12:27, but as with many scriptures, we tend to quote only a part of them. If we look at the last part of that scripture, it says 'that the things which cannot be shaken may remain'. Have you ever wondered what exactly is being shaken and what will remain? Storms and fiery trials are definitely times when we will be shaken, but if there are things which cannot be shaken and will remain, what are they?

As I pondered over the phrase 'unshakable faith', one of the first scriptures the Lord led me to was Matthew 7:24-27. The setting for this particular passage is a mountain. Jesus, having seen the multitudes, went up the mountain and began to teach them. His illustration was about two types of hearers—the obedient and the disobedient. Although both hear God's word, some hear and obey, while others hear but disobey. Both hearers in the illustration proceed to build a house. The wise man builds his house [representing his life], on the words of Jesus, which is the rock. The foolish man builds his house on the sand, and he 'thinks that his house is secure simply because he has heard and acknowledged the words [of God]' (MacArthur, 1985, p. 482). It is worth noting that the foolish man does not intentionally set out to build a house that is likely to fall, nor does he foresee what is likely to happen.

This story which Jesus told, implies that both houses were of a similar style and, therefore, from the outward appearance, they would look very much alike. Both houses were also built in the same general location, and so they experienced the same storm. Although both builders have confidence that their houses will stand the test of time, one trusts in the Lord, while the other trusts in himself and his own works. The main difference between the two was, of course, the foundations upon which they built their respective houses. The wise man built his upon the rock, which is solid, stable, and unmovable. At the same time, the foolish man built his on the sand, which 'by contrast, is loose, unstable and extremely movable' (MacArthur, 1985, p. 482). Nonetheless, if there is one thing in life that each of us is guaranteed, it is that the rain, floods, winds, and storms will beat upon every house!

Matthew Henry (1992) states it so eloquently and clearly when he reminds us that everyone 'has a house to build and that house is our hope of heaven' (p. 1647). Just as the church is built upon the solid rock and foundation of the Lord Jesus, so is every true born-again believer. When the rain, floods and winds come and beat upon the house, that believer is as strong and immovable as a rock. Unsurprisingly, the house which was built upon the sand not only fell in the storm, it collapsed at a time when the builder had most need of it. He had thought and indeed expected his house to be a place of shelter for him in the midst of the fierce storm (Henry, 1992).

The rock spoken of in this passage is, of course, the Lord Jesus. True discipleship is not just about hearing and believing the voice of God; it is about being obedient, believing, and doing what He says. The house on the rock is a picture of a life founded on a proper relationship with Jesus, which will stand the test on the day of judgment. But the house on the sand will fail the test. In Luke's account of this story, the one who listens to and acts on Jesus' teaching can face any difficult circumstance. 'Not acting on Jesus' teaching will cause a person to be overwhelmed by circumstances, eventually resulting in total loss' (Nelson, 2018, p. 1523).

So, to answer the question I started with about what will be shaken, and what will remain, the foundations and structure upon which our beliefs are based will be tested and shaken in the storms and fiery trials of life. But, if they are built upon the rock which is Christ Jesus, they cannot be moved; they will remain. You can therefore have unshakable faith in and stand secure upon the foundation stone and finished work of Jesus through every storm and fiery trial that comes your way.

Testing the genuineness of faith

Hebrews Chapter 11 is often referred to as 'Faith's Hall of Fame' or the 'Hall of faith'. Many of us can most likely quote the first verse of the chapter, which says, 'Now faith is the substance of things hoped for, the evidence of things not seen'. Although we know and believe that scripture, there are still times in our life when we do not or cannot seem to believe or have faith without first either having evidence or receiving a sign of some kind.

It is not clear who the writer of the Hebrews is, but we do know the epistle was addressed to the Jewish Christians who were feeling demoralized and discouraged at that point. Being a Christian had been difficult for them, and many were ready to leave the 'uncharted waters of faith for the comfortable, familiar life of works and moral effort' (Nelson, 2018, p. 1874). The writer of Hebrews reminds those believers of the 'superiority of Jesus' and that:

> *'Faith means we cannot see the outcome, we are not sure what lies ahead. But we are convinced of the reality of God.... Those who do not have faith cannot see past the physical world around them. They are limited by their temporal circumstances and are blind to what God is doing. But those who open their spiritual eyes can see the spiritual realities which transcend this world. Their hope is in God's strength and in His faithfulness. In that hope, they find the strength to endure.... Faith is never easy. But the more convinced we are of the reality of an all-good, all-powerful God, the more our trust will grow and the less we will be overwhelmed by doubts and temptations'* (Nelson, 2018, p. 1874).

Hebrews provides a definition of what faith is and tells us that without faith, it is impossible to please God. In fact, faith wins acceptance and reward from God. When facing storms and fiery trials, we need to endure by faith and are told, 'do not cast away your confidence which has great reward. For you have need of endurance so that after you have done the will of God, you may receive the promise' (Chapter 10:35-36). Furthermore, the book of Hebrews provides an impressive list of famous heroes [both male and female], from the Old Testament, whose stories are exemplary examples of what it means to live by faith. These are intended to encourage us to do the same.

Despite having the Bible, which is God's living word, we vigorously still seek evidence or signs. In their book 'Kneeling we triumph', Edwin and Lillian Harvey (2007) talk about 'faith stripped of human aids' (p. 38).

Unshakable faith

In other words, faith without human assistance, help, or encouragement. That, for many of us, may feel like a step too far. But God wants us to ask in faith, without doubting, and believe in the promises He has spoken to us regarding our situation. When God has given us a promise from Himself, 'we must depend upon the performance of the promise when all the ways leading to it are shut up. We must rejoice in God when we have nothing else to rejoice in and cleave to Him' (Henry, 1992, p. 683).

One of the stories in the Bible which speaks about the genuineness of faith being tested is in Mark 5. There we read about a man called Jairus who was desperately seeking help for his daughter. We are not told what was wrong with his little girl nor how long she had been unwell. Behind the few words that are in the scriptures, there lie all the elements of emerging tragedy for this family. Jairus was a ruler in the synagogue at Capernaum, and he looked after the building, its contents, and the arrangements for worship, but he would not normally take part in it. Holding such a position made Jairus one of the most important and respected men in the community. Here in Mark's gospel, he finds himself in a situation that no parent would ever want to be in. His daughter—his only daughter—at the tender age of twelve is at the point of death. The story is even more heartbreaking because, according to Jewish custom, a girl becomes a woman at the age of twelve. It would be a tragic double blow to Jairus and his wife for their daughter to have reached this significant milestone, only for her to be taken away from them. Because of this situation, Jairus was facing a great trial in his life. This trial was personal, it was emotional, and if the child died, it would be life-changing for his family.

Parenting an unwell child in any situation can feel unbearable, especially when they are younger and cannot tell you what is wrong with them. As a parent, that makes you feel helpless and hopeless because you do not know how best to help or care for them. In our world, today, waiting for an ambulance or a Doctor can feel like an eternity. Imagine a world without medicine or a National Health Service. Hour after hour, Jairus would have listened to those at his home weeping and wailing. Hour after hour, he watched his wife tenderly care for their child, but nothing seemed to be making a difference. Not only has Jairus got his own emotions, but he also has his wife's and possibly those of other family members or friends to cope with as well. In addition to this, Jairus has an even bigger dilemma playing on his mind. He would have known that the Pharisees and priests were looking for any reason whatsoever to arrest Jesus. Seeking help from Jesus would, therefore, potentially put his job and livelihood at stake. However, on the other hand, if he does not go to Jesus for help, his daughter will die.

Jairus may well have questioned why a loving God would allow his family to go through a situation like this in the first place, but there is no mention of that in the scriptures. Sometimes trials and tribulations can be a turning or pivoting point which forces us to address areas in our life that we have been putting off. For example, 'I will go to church next week. I will give my life to Jesus another day. I will wait until after the next office party. I will wait until I am older. I will pray tomorrow'. Before we know it, the years have slipped by, and we have done nothing about it.

It could be assumed that Jairus had previous opportunities to come to Jesus because He was no stranger to the synagogue. In fact, it was His custom and his job to go there. But something stirred within Jairus that particular day, and he was compelled to get up and go in search of Jesus. We should not underestimate the extent of Jairus' decision to leave his wife and their daughter, who was lying in her bed, on the brink of death. One motivating reason for Jairus to do so could be because the little girl was unable to go to Jesus herself and he, as her dad, felt compelled to go on her behalf. Whatever it was, the genuineness of Jairus' faith in Jesus to heal his daughter was being prodded and tested.

What a beautiful picture Mark's gospel paints for us of Jairus' story. Visualise the scene—Jesus has just got off the boat, there is a great multitude around Him, it is noisy and hard to get close to Him. Standing there on the shores of the Sea of Galilee would have been very picturesque with the waves rolling in and the hills in the background, but Jairus' goal was to get to Jesus. He had to lay aside his pride and his prejudice. I imagine his tear-stained face showed the desperation, turmoil, and emotion he was going through, yet he seemed completely oblivious to those around him and his surroundings. Any reservations he once had about approaching Jesus seem to have been lost on his journey along the way. Jairus is a broken man. He has no one and nowhere else to turn. When he finally gets to Jesus, we read that 'he fell at His feet and begged Him earnestly' or, as Matthew's account says, he 'worshipped Him [Jesus]'.

Jairus then asks Jesus to come and lay His hands on his daughter so that she may be healed and live. It may be that Jairus had seen Jesus healing people in this way before, but whatever the reason, he certainly had faith to believe that this was the answer. Jesus did indeed take individuals by the hand, and He transformed their lives. His hand was a healing hand, a life-giving hand, a sight-giving hand, a delivering hand and a guiding hand. His touch was personal. His touch was powerful.

It is also possible that the level of Jairus' faith at that time, was such that he felt Jesus had to be physically present and touch the child in order for her to be healed. How fascinating it is to observe that Jairus was, with all good intentions, stipulating the way in which Jesus was to heal his daughter and resolve his situation! Needless to say, Jesus had other plans which would continue to prod and test the genuineness or the substance of Jairus' faith, especially when it did not happen in the way he thought, or expected it would.

As Jairus and Jesus start walking together towards the place where the child lay, their journey is intercepted by the woman with the issue of blood. I believe this interruption was allowed to challenge and stretch Jairus' faith in preparation for what was about to come. The miraculous healing of the woman would have highlighted to Jairus the authority Jesus had over an illness. That in itself would have been encouraging. It also demonstrated to Jairus that the response of faith not only pleases Jesus, but He honours it. Sometimes situations or people are purposefully and divinely brought across our path to challenge our thinking and stretch our faith.

As all this is going on, Jairus receives the news that it is too late; his daughter has passed away. He was not taken to a private room and invited to take a seat. No, Jairus is told this devastating news publicly in front of a great multitude. While the child was alive, there was hope but it would seem like God's will had been revealed and the matter was determined. You cannot help but feel the rush of emotions and barrage of thoughts that must have gone through Jairus' mind in a split second. He may well have been at a crossroads in his mind about whether to ask Jesus to go any further.

With the natural mind, the outcome of Jairus' situation looked fatal, irreversible, and unable to be remedied (Nelson, 2018). Jesus spoke directly into Jairus' situation and addressed any doubts he may have had. Not only was it an immediate response, it was one of comfort, and reassurance, but also a simple instructional one, 'Do not be afraid, only believe'. However, Jairus still had to make a decision over whether he was going to believe and stand on that word from Jesus or focus on the reality of his situation, which was that his daughter had died.

There are so many lessons to be learned from this story. Had Jairus been focusing purely on his situation, the most important thing for him to do would have been to stay at home. It took courage for Jairus to lay aside those things in his life that demanded his attention and go in search of Jesus. At some point, Jairus possibly realised his personal inability to deal with the situation regarding his child, so he brought it to the feet of Jesus. And there, in the midst of the multitude, Jairus unashamedly falls on his knees and worships Jesus.

What a high honour it is as a parent to stand in the gap for your child when they cannot go to Jesus themselves. Nothing compares to the knowledge that the loved ones you are praying for may have known a different outcome—except—that you stood in the gap for them and paid the price in prayer. How different the outcome would have been for this family had Jairus not gone in search of Jesus. God does not require you to be a perfect parent. Rather, He wants you to be a praying parent and to seek Him in every circumstance. The storm or fiery trial is, therefore, not intended to annihilate you. It tests to see if the genuineness or substance of your faith is founded upon the rock Christ Jesus and whether you will choose to worship Him no matter what you are going through.

Being tested on the genuineness of your faith is difficult because you cannot see the full picture nor how God is working everything out. The Greek term for the word faith means 'trust' or 'firm persuasion', but the corresponding verb means 'to believe'. This is what Jesus was referring to when He said to Jairus 'only believe'. Having faith is about relinquishing trust in yourself and putting that trust in another, namely Jesus (Nelson, 2018).

Jairus' story is a reminder for us in our hardest and darkest days to look for Jesus and keep focused on Him. He can bring good out of any situation no matter how difficult and irreversible it may look in reality. Jesus has a place of peace for you in the midst of your storm and fiery trial, but you must learn to have faith and trust in Him. Yes, there will be a multitude of other voices around you, but holding on to the promises God has given you and hearing His voice, above all the others, is key.

Coming to Jesus in front of the multitude, taking his stand, and walking with Him took courage for Jairus. Likewise, entrusting your most precious treasure, your son or daughter, into God's hands also takes courage. No parent would want their child or family to go through a similar situation to Jairus, but what a testimony this little girl must have had! Imagine opening up your eyes, and the first thing you see is Jesus looking at you with such love and compassion. Or, imagine Jesus holding your hand through your darkest experience.

Regardless of what your situation is with your prodigal child, God is working in your life. He wants you to call on His name and say, 'Lord, show me Your hand in my life'. He wants you to trust that when you are afraid or anxious, you can come to Him and find His peace in the midst of it all. So often, we can become blinded by our circumstances, afraid of what is happening, afraid of the future, discouraged, quick to complain, or become bitter. Our first instinct is not to look for God in the midst of it all. Remember, God is fitting everything together and working it all out for your good even when you cannot see it. Do not give up before you get your breakthrough. Keep pushing through.

Steps in faith

Giving God control over your life and having faith to believe He is able to finish the good work He started in you is an act of your will (Omartian, 2012). Great faith does not give up. It speaks to something which you cannot yet see in the natural, as though it has already happened. Even where situations can look like they are a defeat, they can be a victory, despite your inability to foresee how that could ever be possible. Rest assured in the knowledge that the Lord is the victor because of who He is and what He has accomplished at Calvary. As you hear and receive the word from God for your situation, and stand firm on it, your faith will increase. God wants you to stay focused on what He has led you to do. His desire is that you allow Him to lead you through your storm and fiery trial, step-by-step, in faith.

I heard a story some time ago about a father and daughter who had a car journey to make. The weather forecast had indicated that a storm was coming, and as the daughter was a fairly new driver, she suggested to her dad that he should drive. He insisted that she drive and reassured her that he would be right there with her. Sure enough, the storm came, and at times, it was almost impossible for the daughter to see where she was going with the heavy rain, fog, and spray from other vehicles. The daughter, on several occasions, asked her dad if she should stop and pull over like the other vehicles on the road, but he kept telling her to keep going. Eventually, they drove through the storm. After pulling over, the father asked his daughter to look back, and he asked her where the other vehicles were. She replied that they were still in the storm!

We have, in our storms and fiery trials, what looks like a justified reason to stop and pull over because we cannot see where we are going. Similarly, when your child heads into the far country, it is tempting and a natural instinct to pull over and stop doing what God has called you to do, but that is not what He desires. He wants you to keep going, one step at a time, and He has promised to be right there with you. It is not His will that you should be stuck and immobilised in the storm or fiery trial. Stay focused and committed to the Lord's work even though it may feel like the last thing you should do, or want to do.

Finding a quiet place and time every day can be difficult during normal times, but even more so during stormy times and fiery trials. When you can, you will find a release in being able to offload your worries, anxieties, and fears to Jesus, knowing He is waiting and wanting to hear from you. The Holy Spirit wants to fellowship and partner with you each step of this journey. As you sit in His presence, draw close to Him and commit everything into His hands. It is a great opportunity to remind yourself of the promises and words God has given you regarding your own life and your prodigal child's.

In the presence of God, negative thoughts and anxieties begin to fade as you worship Him for who He is. Faith begins to rise in the knowledge and reassurance that God is still in control. No matter what the situation looks like in the flesh, or which voices seem to be filling your head with words that are contrary to God's, your faith in Jesus will start to build up gradually. Pray and begin to embrace the plan and purposes God has for your life, knowing He is working all things together for your good. Faith is saying, 'I have confidence in God that He is bigger than this giant' of fear which has already been defeated (Giglio, 2017, p. 65). Most importantly, remember that 'without faith, it is impossible to please Him, for he who comes to God must believe that He is, and that He is a rewarder of those who diligently seek Him' (Hebrews 11:6).

Hearing the voice of God speaking to you through His word or some other means, will change your perspective on your situation. By taking steps in faith, you can confidently silence the negative voices with the word and promises of God in your storm or fiery trial. Then as fear would try to rise up from the depths of your stomach, immobilise you and begin to play out all kinds of scenarios in your mind, you can lean into the truths of God's word and promises to you. God is able. He is limitless. God is the only one who can save. He is the only one who can turn your situation around, and He can do it in the twinkling of an eye.

Antidote to fear

There have been numerous times over the last few years where I have felt like I was living under what I described earlier as a 'heavy defeatist atmosphere and fog of hopelessness'. Initially, it was really hard to identify my feelings and pinpoint exactly what was going on in my head. Yes, God had given me promises, and I knew I was hearing His voice more clearly. I also knew my faith was rooted firmly in the Lord and that He is the victor in this battle. Yet despite all that, I felt defeated in it all, and that brought feelings of fear, anxiety, and a heaviness. For a variety of reasons, I could not see a way through the fog.

As I sought the Lord, He led me to the story of Gideon in the book of Judges. We first catch up with Gideon when he is threshing wheat in a winepress, which was a square or circular pit, carved into the rock and used for crushing grapes. It should be noted that wheat would normally be threshed on an open floor [not in a winepress] to allow the wind to carry away the chaff in the winnowing process.

By way of background, God had promised to increase Israel, but their growth had stopped because they had done evil in the sight of the Lord and had returned to idolatry and worshiping false gods. Because of that, God allowed the Israelites to be delivered into the hand of the Midianites, and they came upon them as a multitude of grasshoppers to plunder the country and enrich themselves with its spoils (Henry, 1992). Rather than fight or retaliate, the Israelites imprisoned themselves in dens and caves because of their own faintheartedness. One of the strategies which the Midianites used was to leave the Israelites in peace while they sowed seeds for the crops. Then when harvest time came, they would come back, seize it all, eat or destroy the produce, take away the sheep and oxen, and leave Israel with no sustenance. For seven years, this went on, year after year, until finally, Israel cried to the Lord once more.

Although Gideon was a brave man with an active spirit, he was weak in faith, and his courage failed him (Henry, 1992). On the day that the angel of the Lord appeared to him under the terebinth tree, he was hiding from the Midianites in the winepress. The angel said to him, 'The Lord is with you, you mighty man of valor' (Judges 6:12). Gideon questioned angel's statement because he assumed God could not possibly be with him because of all the things that were happening to Israel. The fact that Gideon did not feel the Lord with him did not mean that He was not. Similarly, when things are going wrong for us, we likewise assume we must be out of the will of God and He is not with us. Gideon's starting point, therefore, seems to have been from a position of defeat and powerlessness, especially as he considers himself to be the least of his father's house and his clan to be the weakest in Manasseh.

It was while Gideon was alone, away from the noise and busyness of life, that the angel of the Lord appeared and told him that God was going to use him to deliver Israel. God gave Gideon the necessary qualifications and reassurance to carry out this assignment. As He calls him valiant, which means courageous, so He made him—it was not something Gideon already had. The conversation with the angel not only revived Gideon's spirit but also silenced his fears (Henry, 1992). Gideon received a promise that the Lord would be with him to guide and strengthen him, he would not die, and the assignment would be successful. God also provided very clear step-by-step instructions on what Gideon was to do next. He was definitely not to go in his own might or strength. Neither was he to depend on his own valour. Rather, Gideon was instructed to go in the might and strength he received from the Lord.

Gideon's first assignment to remove the altar of Baal was just a foretaste of what was to come. In his second assignment, we again get a glimpse into the way the Lord led Gideon through this, whilst recognising his fears and providing exactly the right information he needed to dispel them. In Chapter 7, we read, 'It happened on the same night that the Lord said to him, 'Arise, go down against the camp, for I have delivered it into your hand. But if you are *afraid* to go down, go down to the camp with Purah, your servant, and you shall hear what they say; and afterward, your hands shall be strengthened to go down against the camp" (vs. 9-11). When Gideon got to the camp, he heard a man telling a dream to his companion, who then interpreted it and said that the Lord had delivered Midian and the whole camp into Gideon's hand. When Gideon heard the dream and its interpretation, 'he worshipped' God.

Experiencing fear during your storm or fiery trial can be perfectly normal. However, it is not God's intention that your storm or fiery trial should cause you to hide away or imprison yourself in fear and anxiety. The lesson you can learn from Gideon's story is that you may feel like you are starting from the point of defeat because of the enormity and seriousness of the situation, but if you could see the overall picture, you would see that God is the victor and He is with you. Your unshakable faith comes from spending time alone with God, listening to His voice, obediently following His direction and holding on to the word and promises of God with every step you take. Then you, too, can rise in confidence and get on with the task set before you, regardless of how frightening or impossible it looks.

'Faith is the antidote to fear', and the 'soundtrack of faith is worship' (Giglio, 2017, p. 65-75). It might feel hard initially and out of context to praise God in your situation, particularly when you are battling with underlying fears and the outcome of your storm and fiery trial is not yet clear. But that is exactly the right time because putting on the garment of praise, especially when the spirit of heaviness would try to overpower you, will confuse the enemy and dispel your anxieties. 'Worship and worry cannot occupy the same space... One displaces the other' (Giglio, 2017, p. 74).

Knowing and having confidence that God is in control of your situation will help your fears to dissipate and your faith to build and rise. Begin to grasp the reality that the battle is not yours to solve, and you do not need to carry the burden of it nor the associated fear that comes with it. The battle belongs to the Lord, and He is well in control of it. The more you focus on Him, the more you will stand firm on the rock and not be shaken in your faith or overwhelmed by fears. Soon you will realise that the difficult circumstances and storms are used by the Lord to build you up in your faith.

Facing your fears and stepping out in faith on the word God has spoken to you may not seem like the most sensible thing to do, especially when the way ahead is not clear, and there are so many other things you feel need to be remedied beforehand. You may even want to wait until you personally feel in a good place and are starting from a place of strength. During those times, listen to the voice of God, who He says you are, and what He is asking you to do. Then and only then, take the next step in faith, no matter how strange or fearful it may appear. Remember, it is about being obedient to what God is asking you to do rather than the actual act itself. He will lead and guide you through the storms and the fog.

Building your faith

Taking steps in faith and realising your storms and fiery trials are used by God, will help you to keep going through difficult times. As you allow Him to strengthen you in your weakness, you will learn to trust in God and not yourself. Building your faith is a process that grows in wilderness experiences. It makes me think about how the Israelites must have felt in Exodus 14 when they were sandwiched between the Red Sea before them, and the armies of Pharaoh coming behind them. Yet the word from the Lord to Moses was to go forward, 'do not be afraid. Stand still and see the salvation of the Lord which He will accomplish for you today' (vs. 13). The situation the Israelites found themselves in seemed so hopeless, and they would have been ill-equipped to fight against the armies of Pharaoh. They must have questioned the accuracy of the words and instructions given by God to Moses. Standing still, knowing it would only be a matter of time before Pharaoh's armies arrived, would have been an extremely hard and frightening thing to do. Yet they had nowhere to run or to hide. Neither had they any alternative but to stand still and have faith in what God said.

I have stood at the water's edge looking out across the sea and wondered what it must have been like for Moses to be faced with a vast area of water before him, Pharaoh's armies fast approaching from behind, and have the responsibility of a few million people's lives in between. Moses must surely have questioned his credentials for such a task especially given that the Israelites considered the sea to be an uncontrollable enemy. Once more, God was faithful and gave Moses specific instructions at the right time. He was to stretch out his hand over the sea and divide it. God used its parting as a demonstration to Moses and the Israelites that every force in creation was under His control (Nelson, 2018).

I have also wondered what it must have been like to walk on the dry sea bed with two massive walls of water on either side. What a surreal situation to experience, but it shows us how God made a way when there was no way. Not only that, He gave the Israelites such words of comfort and reassurance beforehand when He said, 'The Lord will fight for you, and you shall hold your peace' (Exodus 14:14). The Israelites saw the impossible become possible in front of their very eyes because of God's mighty power. It was nothing to do with human strength or abilities. Their role was merely to walk step-by-step in faith and obedience, following the instruction of Almighty God.

What rich lessons we can learn in our storms and fiery trials. We, too, need to learn to stand still, wait on directions from the Lord and let Him fight for us. It can be hard to accept and understand that there is a divine purpose in the storm and fiery trial, but you need to trust and believe in God's plan for your life even when you cannot trace it. So even when the seas roar and the wind blow you about in the storm, your faith can be unshakable because your foundations have been built upon the rock, and you have learned to trust God no matter what. The word and promises of God will sustain you, and the Holy Spirit will lead, guide, and give you comfort. You will know His peace which passes all understanding because your faith is not in yourself and your ability or even responsibility to change the situation. Your faith is built on Christ the rock.

George Muller once said, 'The beginning of anxiety is the end of faith, and the beginning of true faith is the end of anxiety'.[5] How true that statement is. Our anxieties are caused and heightened when we assess our situations without God. If we are living in anxiety, then we are not walking in faith. 'Quiet tension is not trust. It is simply compressed anxiety' (Dillow, 2007, p. 126).

Although no one likes the wilderness seasons or the storms and fiery trials, faith cannot grow without them. Faith builds and develops in the hardships of trials and what feels like the darkest periods of your life. It is only God and Him alone that can bring something good out of apparent hopelessness. Despite feeling like the wilderness experience, storms, and fiery trials are never going to end. Psalm 30 brings reassurance that 'weeping may endure for a night, but joy comes in the morning' (vs. 5).

The word of God challenges us to draw near to Him with a 'true heart in full assurance of faith' (Hebrews 10:22). The word 'true' in this scripture is derived from the word aléthés, which means unconcealed, not hidden, undeniable reality when something is fully tested. The word 'faith' in the same verse comes from the word peithó and means to be persuaded of what is trustworthy. The next verse bids us to 'hold fast the confession of our hope without wavering, for He who promised is faithful' (vs. 23). Using the root meanings of some of these words, a summary of the two verses would read something like this. 'Let us approach with an unconcealed heart, persuaded of what is trustworthy.... let us hold

---

5. https://www.georgemuller.org/quotes/the-end-of-anxiety

fast an agreement of our hope or expectation, without wavering, unbending, for He who promised is faithful, reliable'.

Building your faith in God looks different on paper from how it does in reality. It is one thing to say and even to write about building your faith in God. However, the real test comes when you have to put that into action and apply it to your situation, your child(ren), and your loved ones. Having faith in God and trusting Him is not wishful thinking. It is knowing that the promises God has given you still stand. His yes is still yes even when the battle is intense, and the level of opposition against the promises is so fierce that you question whether you have actually heard correctly from the Lord. It is knowing in your heart that if He said He would do it, then He will do it. Your role is to 'hold fast' and not waver or bend from what He has said. The darkest times in your life are where God develops you into the person He wants you to be. As you keep persevering and enduring through those times, God 'gives you the credentials to walk into the daylight, having earned the right to be there. Night faith is tenacious, radical and relentless' (Gass, 2005, February 6). If God said it and if He promised it, He cannot lie. His word is true, and you can hold fast to that.

Choices

As we come to the end of Chapter 4, you have a choice over how you view your storms and fiery trials. Choosing to view your situation through the lens of disappointment is one option. Other options would be to feel anxious, fearful, let down, or even unhappy and angry with God. Alternatively, you can choose to submit to the plans and purposes God has for your life, knowing that He has the bigger picture and is weaving everything together beautifully and miraculously for your good. You are not being asked to ignore the pain, disappointment and hurt you feel. Neither are you to be unaware of the pressures, dangers and seriousness of the situation going on around you nor pretend they are not happening.

You can choose to encourage yourself in the Lord and not doubt that He is in control of your situation even though the way it works out may be different from your expectations, timescales and, indeed, what you have asked Him for. The things God has spoken over your life and your child's life will come to pass. Begin to recognise and believe what He has said regarding your situation. Carry those promises with you and voice them often to reinforce them in your own heart and mind. They will give you a tremendous sense of comfort and peace as well as help to build your faith. Most of all, remember that God keeps His word. You can depend on it, and you can depend on Him.

Making a choice not to apportion blame on your partner, other family members, friends, or indeed leaders around you is important. Neither is this the time to look back and long for the 'good old days' as the Israelites did. Rather, you are being asked to keep looking forward, keep your eyes fixed on Jesus, and know there is a reason and purpose for this storm and fiery trial. It will test the genuineness of your faith, but as you observe the ways in which God works to position you for what He has ahead, you will see His abounding love towards you, His faithfulness, and His power to overcome every situation.

Going back to Moses and the Israelites at the edge of the Red Sea, it is interesting to note that they had to purposefully choose to step into the water. Nothing happened until they physically took that step of faith. Likewise, you need to choose whether you are going to step into the next level of faith in your walk with God. F. B. Meyer once said, 'Unbelief puts our circumstances between God and us, but faith puts God between us and our circumstances'.[6] God is looking for those who will choose to put their faith in Him and partner with Him.

God does not intend that you should go forward in your own might. You are to go forward in the strength of the Lord, knowing the battle is not yours. It belongs to the Lord, and therefore you can rest secure in the knowledge that He is able, He is enough, and He is all you need. As you release the future outcomes of your prodigal child to the Lord, you can focus your thinking on His sovereign plan for your life. God will not only give you songs in the night but 'anthems for the dark night of the soul where worry and stress and fear lurk about' (Giglio, 2017, p. 75).

---

6. https://www.azquotes.com/author/19129-F_B_Meyer

Unshakable faith

The foundations upon which your faith is built will only truly be revealed in the storm. During sunny days, the foundations of your faith will, from the outward appearance, look to be steadfast. When the storm comes, you have a choice over whose voice you will listen to. Other voices around you will say things like your situation is not changing, it is getting worse; God has forgotten and abandoned you, or He has not kept His promises. Those voices will even question if you are sure that you have actually heard from God and whether He is able or going to keep His word. It is as though the devil himself or his angels are harassing and bombarding your mind over the authenticity of the promises and God's word. But you and only you have the ability to choose whose report and whose voice you will believe—the words and promises of God which brings hope and life—or the lies of the enemy which brings defeat and hopelessness.

Overcoming the question in your mind as to why you have been allowed to go through this particular storm and fiery trial can be hard. Understanding what is happening and the lessons God wants you and your prodigal child to learn, will help you stand strong during these times. You have this opportunity to grow spiritually in adversity and through being the parent of a prodigal child. Or you can allow it to distract you and throw you off course.

To give in is to say that God is not able to bring you through, that this trial is too hard for Him to hold and sustain you through it and work everything around for your good. That is simply a lie from the devil himself. God is enough. He is able to bring you through. He is all you need during the darkest days of your life.

God continually reminds us through scripture that He is faithful and that He will fulfil every single promise He makes. God cannot lie. He cannot fail. He never changes. He is always the same, at all times, in all circumstances and throughout every generation. If you are in any doubt, have a look at just a few of the scriptures that speak about His promises:

> *'Therefore know that the Lord your God, He is God, the faithful God who keeps covenant and mercy for a thousand generations with those who love Him and keep His commandments'* (Deuteronomy 7:9).

> *'Forever, O Lord, Your word is settled in heaven. Your faithfulness endures to all generations'* (Psalm 119:89-90).
>
> *'No temptation has overtaken you except such as is common to man; but God is faithful, who will not allow you to be tempted beyond what you are able, but with the temptation will also make the way of escape, that you may be able to bear it'* (1 Corinthians 10:13).
>
> *'He who calls you is faithful, who also will do it'* (1 Thessalonians 5:24).

Worshiping the name of Jesus with all of your heart and mind in the midst of turmoil is a choice. By doing so, you will become aware or be reminded of what an amazing God you serve and of His mighty power to do the impossible and make a way when there is no way. Every worry and anxiety will fade into insignificance as you truly worship. Being in the presence of God will renew and refresh your mind and body. Worshipping God is not something you do only when everything in your life is going well. 'We worship because we have learned to trust in God and to praise Him no matter what life throws at us' (Conlon, 2018, p. 243).

You may be wondering how you can possibly thank and worship God when your situation is so dire. Or maybe you think you will wait until circumstances change, and then you will thank Him. No matter what thoughts have spun around your head, God wants you to continue to praise and worship Him through it all. If you are struggling, begin by thanking Him for all the things He has done for you so far and for His faithfulness to the generations that have gone before you. Thank Him that just as He was in the fire alongside Shadrach, Meshach, and Abednego, so He will be with you. Thank Him that as He was with Moses and the children of Israel, so He will be with you. Thank Him for His precious word that leads and guides your every move and never goes out of date. Thank Him for His love for you, your family, and your prodigal child. Thank Him that He has got your situation in control no matter how it looks.

Sitting in the presence of God is a safe place. It is a place where you can tell Him all about the thoughts, fears and anxieties that run through your head that you do not wish to share or even vocalise aloud to anyone else. While everyday burdens, storms, and fiery trials would endeavour to weigh you down and crush you, they can be left at the feet of Jesus in prayer. There in the presence of God, you will find that He will give you the courage and strength to carry on. The peace you find in His presence will make it hard to leave.

Have confidence in God and stand firm in the storm. Regardless of how fierce the wind blows and whichever voices echo around you, rest in the faithfulness of God even when it does not make sense to do so. Never forget that God is awesome. He can move mountains. He can make a way when there seems to be no way. He leads and directs you in the valleys just as much as He does on the mountaintop.

It is empowering to know that you are not alone in your storm or fiery trial, and you can have unshakable faith throughout. I will leave you with the words of this song by Hillsong United called 'Another in the Fire'.[vii]

'There was another in the fire
Standing next to me
There was another in the waters
Holding back the seas

And should I ever need reminding
Of how I've been set free
There is a cross that bears the burden
Where another died for me
There is another in the fire'.

Chapter 5

Purifying process in the refiner's fire

'The believer needs not fear the fiery trial of afflictions and temptations, by which the Saviour refines His gold. He will take care it is not more intense or longer than is needful for his good'.[7]

(Malachi 3:2)

Throughout my Christian life, I have come through various testing times and seasons, all of which have been of different intensity. And although I know that to measure the strength of anything, it must undergo a testing process, it still does not make that period any easier or indeed any more palatable! While there are areas in our life that we may be aware of that need to be refined, there are others that are less obvious and go undetected. Hindsight does allow us to look back through previous testing times and see the ways in which God guided and led us each step of the way and the work He accomplished in our lives through it all. Yet each testing period still seems to come as a shock to the system, not least

---

7. https://biblehub.com/commentaries/mhc/malachi/3.htm

because of the intensity of the last one but also because the whole process can feel lengthy and prolonged.

Partnering with the Holy Spirit and allowing Him to lead you into a new era of empowerment and depth of intimacy requires you to know and live the word of God and walk in obedience to it by faith. Measuring and testing the strength of that and removing anything that is likely to contaminate it or which is not pure is an essential and unavoidable process. If that is where you feel you are at right now, you are not alone or unique.

Different scriptures in the Old Testament refer to 'being tested in the furnace of affliction' as part of a purifying process in the refiner's fire. Understanding the purpose of that purifying process and the refiner's fire in your life is necessary to provide clarity in your storm or fiery trial. You may, of course, feel like you did not need to be purified or refined in this area in the first place.

The book of Malachi uses the two images of 'refiner's fire' and 'launderer's soap' as vivid illustrations of the purifying process. The refiner's fire 'separates between the gold and the dross by melting the ore' while the launderer's soap, with much rubbing, 'fetches the spots out of the cloth' (Henry, 1992, p. 1602). Jesus is, of course, the great refiner, and He purifies His people by purging them as gold and silver. He sanctifies or purifies His people inwardly 'to make them a precious people to Himself' (Henry, 1992, p. 1602). Both of these purifying processes enable God's people to worship Him 'according to His will… that they may be true worshippers, who worship the Father in spirit and in truth' (Henry, 1992, p. 1602).

Purifying is a process in itself, and it takes time for the dross, minerals or anything that contaminates it to be removed. The intensity of the fire is needed for the impurities to rise to the surface so that they can then be taken away. One reason God purges His people through affliction is, as has been mentioned before, so that the 'genuineness of your faith…. may be found to praise, honour and glory at the revelation of Jesus Christ' (1 Peter 1:7). Dixon, in his book 'Elijah's God and Mine' says, 'when faith is tried, it either goes into action and proves God and the sufficiency of His grace, or it collapses' (1978, p. 32). When faith collapses, you become confused and disillusioned during the shaking, purifying and refining process. Another reason for the purifying process is so that the church can be reformed. God does this through His word [The Bible] and His Spirit working with the church to revive and cleanse souls.[8]

In order to grow and mature in the things of God and to have that deeper intimate walk with Him, the purifying and refining process is an unavoidable one. Only then can God as your creator, begin to set and position you as that pure gold into the structure He wants you to be. The whole process is not a pleasant experience but it is very much a worthwhile one! There will continue to be areas in your heart that need to be purified and God will put His finger on these at various times, and thus the purification is ongoing. The process itself takes place on the inside of a person as God undertakes that cleansing and purifies your heart from things you may or may not realise were even there in the first place.

Pursuing God's heart

During the purifying and refining process, you need to pursue God's heart rather than your own desires and wants. While you may be longing for answers and to understand why all of this is being allowed to happen, focusing on that takes you away from the real work God is doing in and through it all. This purifying and refining process is a time to surrender your heart and life again on the altar and allow God to realign and position you so that you can go forward in the power and anointing of the Holy Spirit. The purifying and refining process is not a time to focus on what you think or feel is or is not taking place in your life. As mentioned earlier, the shaking process has a purpose but so too does the purifying and refining process. Nothing happens by chance to those who love the Lord. God is always working in and through you even when it may feel like the darkest time of your life or indeed that nothing at all is happening.

The hardship and all the things Job went through left him confused and mixed up in his mind and thinking. Job was desperate to present his case before the Lord but everywhere he looked he could not seem to catch

---

8. Ibid.

a glimpse or view of Him. It felt to Job that God was at a distance and frowning upon him. Despite all that, he continued to express his faith and assurance in God. Job declared, 'But He knows the way that I take; When He has tested me, I shall come forth as gold' (Chapter 23:10). If you know God is working in your life in a particular way, and if you are willing to trust Him, 'faith, not presumption, will never be disappointed' (Dixon, 1978, p. 36). God is taking you to that place of deeper trust with Himself and it is important during this time that you stay close to Him and His word. By doing so, you too will come forth as pure gold.

Trusting God through the purifying and refining process and pursuing His heart will strengthen and prove the genuineness of your faith. 'Some forms of worship only release their sweetest fragrance to God when offered from the fires of trials and adversity. The sacrifice of praise offered in times of trouble is especially sweet and pleasant to the King of Kings. This is worship from a posture of trust and faith instead of suspicion and doubts' (Tenney, 2003, p. 25). Furthermore, trusting God in the midst of the purifying and refining process not only influences others it will also encourage them as they witness the evident faithfulness and grace of God in your life.

Knowing there is a divine purpose for the purifying and refining process and that you are right in the centre of God's will for your life brings stability to your situation. Pursuing God's heart, allowing Him to purify and refine the impurities and anything that would keep you back from fulfilling the plans He has for your life, will also bring focus and purpose. Then as you begin to see the bigger picture, you will be able to rest in the knowledge that the testimony of what God has done in your life will bring glory to His name. You will become steadfast, unshakeable and firmly rooted on the rock which is Christ Jesus. Other people may not be able to understand what is happening in your life nor indeed see any purpose or value in it because they will only be aware of the external hardship and challenges you are experiencing rather than the work God is doing internally in your heart and life.

Avoiding the purifying and refining process seems like an attractive option and a way of swerving a lot of pain. But if you do not go through the process, you will miss out on seeing and experiencing the supernatural ways in which God holds and leads you through those times. God has promised to do a new thing and make a road in the wilderness and rivers in the desert. In order for that to happen, you must choose and accept His plan rather than making your own direction in life. For that purpose alone, it is important not to resist the purifying and refining process God is doing in you.

Everything God has allowed you to go through is bringing you to a place where you will eventually be able to see its purpose and know deep inside that it was all worthwhile. God will do something beautiful through it because He has promised to work all things together for your good and He cannot lie. It is definitely worth persevering during the purifying and refining process. You will be surprised beyond measure and it will be far better than anything you could ever have imagined. Walk with Him step-by-step into the fullness of what He has for you. Do not try to hold on to anything that God puts His finger on in the purifying and refining process. Allow yourself to be x-rayed by the Holy Spirit and strive for that clean, pure heart.

Learning lessons in the purifying and refining process

You never know what a day is going to bring, nor what events are likely to unfold. While your best-intended plans will, on occasions, go ahead as envisioned, at other times, they may not. In Matthew 26, we read that preparations were underway across Jerusalem to celebrate the Passover. Jewish families were required to stay within the boundaries of Jerusalem itself and families had a number of customs and tasks to undertake. These included: cleaning the house and removing any leavened bread; baking unleavened bread; taking the lamb to the temple to be prepared for the feast; mashing apples, dates, pomegranates and nuts into a paste called charosheth; and preparing a collection of bitter herbs. The meal or Last Supper as it was known, was then traditionally served early in the evening.

After celebrating the Passover, Jesus and the disciples sang a hymn before then heading to the Mount of Olives. This was not a random walk in the early evening moonlight after a heavy meal, it had all been pre-planned. The location itself is interesting not least because 'Gethsemane' is only mentioned twice in the Bible, but because Jerusalem is a city set on a hilltop and there was little or no room for open spaces. Only wealthy citizens had private gardens on the Mount of Olives. Who the owner of the garden was or how Jesus came to have access to it, we are not told. But we do know that Jesus met there often with His disciples.

On arrival at the Mount of Olives, Jesus asks some of the disciples to wait while He takes Peter, James and John deeper into the garden and shares with them that His 'soul is exceedingly sorrowful even to death' (Matthew 26:38). You would think that such words would have provoked a reaction but the events and drama over the last few days had caused the disciples to be overcome with physical fatigue at the cost of spiritual awareness.

When we think about Jesus praying, we often have a vision that it is very reverent, controlled and somewhat peaceful. That may have been the case on certain occasions but not on this particular day. The writer of Hebrews talks about Jesus praying in the garden with vehement or intense cries and tears. Commentators suggest that Jesus' cries were so loud that the disciples who were further away heard them. Jesus falls on His face, not in an act of drama but His lying prostrate on the ground begins to tell the unspoken story of the agony and extremity of His sorrow. Such extreme spiritual anguish must have had an impact on His mental, emotional and physical condition and wellbeing.

During His years of ministry, Jesus talked about Calvary with His disciples. He knew it was going to happen. Yet in this passage of scripture, the first prayer we initially read seems somewhat strange. Jesus asks His Father, 'if it is possible, let this cup pass from me'. A cup in the Bible is a common symbol of a person's destiny in life, and a bitter cup symbolizes trials and hardship. After spending an hour in prayer, Jesus comes back to find the disciples sleeping. During the second and third prayer times, we see Jesus surrendering Himself to the Father and so His prayer changes to 'not as I will, but as You will' (vs. 39-44).

Returning after the third prayer time, Jesus singles Peter out and tells him to 'watch and pray lest you enter into temptation. The spirit is willing but the flesh is weak'. Luke's gospel gives us an even closer insight

Purifying process in the refiner's fire

into the conversation whereby Jesus also tells Peter, 'satan has asked for you that he may sift you as wheat. But I have prayed for you that your faith should not fail; and when you have returned to me, strengthen your brethren' (Chapter 22:31).

When Peter woke up that morning, he would never have anticipated how his day was going to unfold. To him it was another celebration of the Passover and he knew the various routines that needed to be undertaken in preparation for the evening meal. Peter must have wondered why Jesus was saying those words to him and what He meant by them. However, as the events of the evening began to unfold, Peter's world was turned upside down. One minute Peter is in the presence of Jesus, doing His work and the next, he finds himself in the middle of a crisis. Firstly, he is confronted by soldiers in a garden which was supposedly a place of solitude and prayer. Then he finds himself in the courtyard of the high priest, where he denies the Lord Jesus with oaths and curses. Fear would have made Peter want to run, but His love for Jesus kept him there. Even after he denies Jesus the second time, he is still there. It is only after the cock crows the third time that Peter goes out into the night and weeps bitterly.

Sometimes there is no hint or warning that the purifying and refining process is coming your way. A crisis can threaten your peace by protruding into your life uninvited. As a Christian, you are not exempt from a crisis, no matter how close you are to Jesus. God knows you will let Him down but He is waiting on you returning to Him. He has a plan for your life and He will provide the instructions for the next step you are to take. Do not ask God to take you out of the purifying and refining process. Ask for His grace to bear it well. Process is important and you will not learn the lessons God has for you if you are taken out of it. The purifying and refining process is intended to remove the impurities, deepen your relationship with God, grow your faith and draw you closer to Him.

The purifying process was never intended to destroy or consume you. God is doing a work in you but He is also changing others around you. Of course, the purifying process in the refiner's fire is hard but God will reward you and make something beautiful out of it. This is the season to allow God the time and space to refine, prepare and position you for all that He has planned and promised you. There is no shortcut in the purifying and refining process. It must go through specific stages for a reason and these things take a certain amount of time!

Resisting the temptation to become bitter

Change, which can be uncomfortable, is an inherent part of the purifying process as you progress through the refiner's fire. Not knowing how God is working everything out for your good, being unable to clearly see the end results, and having no defined end date are all frustrations of the purifying and refining process. The refiner's fire is, however, the place where God wants to deal with you as a person. Being the parent of a prodigal child makes the purifying and refining process feel more challenging, particularly because there are now two different processes going on—one with you and one with your prodigal child. Watching your child go deeper into the things of the world is excruciatingly painful for a Christian parent. So, it is only natural to want God to sort that out first and deal with you later.

The suddenness of finding yourself in the refiner's fire, along with the severity of change it brings with it is distressing. If you are not careful, it can be easy to allow bitterness and resentment to creep in because of the intensity and prolonged duration of the purifying and refining process.

You have a choice over how you respond to the purifying and refining process. Going through the refiner's fire yourself while coping with your prodigal child may feel unbearable and crushing, particularly as it seems ill-timed and also because of the extreme intensity of the whole situation. You can choose to try and hold on to the things that God is putting His finger on in your life. Or you can lay down your own dreams, desires and ambitions for yourself and your child and allow God to do the work He has planned in both of you.

Letting go in the refiner's fire is such a battle not least because of the need to feel in control of situations and be seen to be dealing with them. Not dealing with situations, or at least not trying to address or prevent them from escalating, conflicts with your role as a parent. Relinquishing control in the refiner's fire aligns with feelings of failure, responsibility avoidance or appearing too busy and caught up in ministry to step aside

Purifying process in the refiner's fire

and focus on family matters. Letting go and entrusting your prodigal child's life to God is therefore easily confused with giving up on them voluntarily, allowing them to be sifted as wheat by satan and released to an unknown destiny and eternal fate.

1 Samuel 1 tells the story of Elkanah the Ephraimite, who was married to Hannah. When Hannah could not bear children, Elkanah took a second wife called Peninnah because failure to have children in ancient Israel was regarded as a tragedy. Blame for not having children was, in those days, assigned to the woman and her barrenness could be the cause for divorce (Nelson, 2018).

Elkanah's decision to have two wives was an accepted social custom but it caused division in this particular family. Peninnah was fruitful and she was blessed with many sons and daughters. Hannah, on the other hand, was barren but she was very dear to her husband and he openly let her and others know how he felt about her.

'Peninnah could not bear the blessing of fruitfulness…. Hannah could not bear the affliction of barrenness', and so she grew sad and discontented (Henry, 1992, p. 381). To make things worse, Peninnah provoked Hannah severely because of her barrenness. She also envied the love that Elkanah had for Hannah. The more kindness Elkanah showed Hannah, the more infuriated Peninnah became.

Each year Elkanah would take his family to the house of the Lord. Year after year, Peninnah would use this opportunity to provoke Hannah the most about being barren. She used taunting language and referred to her 'as one whom heaven did not favour' (Henry, 1992, p. 381). It is not clear from the scripture how long this provocation had been going on, nor exactly the reason why. Perhaps Peninnah wanted to try to break Hannah's heart so that she could solely gain Elkanah's attention and his heart. Or, possibly Peninnah simply took great pleasure in making Hannah uneasy and fretful. Regardless of the reason, while all that was taking place in the background, Elkanah would do his best to try to comfort, encourage and show his affection to Hannah. He even suggested to Hannah that his love for her was a greater blessing than having ten sons.

Biblical accounts such as this one, allow us to see that 'husbands and wives whose future children were predestined to be patriarchs, and prophets, and judges, and forerunners of Jesus Christ in the house of Israel, began their married life with having no children' (White, 1952, p. 207). We can only make well-intended assumptions and propose suggested reasons as to why that was the case because the Bible does not tell us. However, what we do know is that it was the Lord who closed Hannah's womb and He had a reason and purpose for doing so.

During those intense years, Hannah could never have imagined that one day she would have a son who would be mighty in the sight of God and that he would hear God speaking to him as a young child. Neither did she envisage that she would have more than one child. In her purifying and refining process, she could not have foreseen how God was working it all together for good. All she could see and feel were the facts and the reality of the situation which was that she did not have children and she was suffering greatly at the hands of her adversary Peninnah, who made her life a misery.

All this trouble and years of provoking finally had an impact on Hannah's appetite. The changes in Hannah were so drastic, that they had become outwardly noticeable to her husband. When Elkanah gently chided Hannah for her inordinate grief, she did not harden her heart or become bitter, even despite her great sorrow. Rather, she did her best to cheer herself up and come to the table to eat.

The story goes on and we read that Hannah and her family were 'at Shiloh, at the door of the tabernacle, where God had promised to meet His people and which was the house of prayer' (Henry 1992, p. 381). Having offered their peace offerings, they had feasted on the sacrifice and it was proper and timely that she put up her prayer to the Lord. Hannah's prayers were so earnest yet so mingled with tears. She wept sore and was in total anguish. The scripture says she was in 'bitterness of soul', which simply means she was discontented or dissatisfied with her circumstances, and they weighed heavy on her. Yet just as those tears flowed freely from her eyes, so did the prayer that flowed from the depths of her heart. Verse 12 of 1 Samuel 1 says Hannah 'continued praying before the Lord', which suggests she said more than what has been recorded for us in this passage of scripture. It was a simple, specific prayer in which she petitioned the Lord for a man-child.

Purifying process in the refiner's fire

Hannah did not start shouting at the Lord or blaming Him for her situation and for not giving her children. Rather, she prayed so softly that no one could hear her. Hannah had no desire or ulterior motive for her earnest, fervent prayer to be seen or heard by those around her. Anyone observing nearby would only have seen her lips move but she knew God saw her heart. He knew her thoughts and the desires she had for a child. Although her prayer was uttered from the secret place of her heart, the location where she prayed was quite the opposite. It was a very public place.

This would not have been the first time Hannah had prayed to the Lord. She had been in the house of the Lord before and would have prayed. Although scripture does not tell us, it could be that in the past, Hannah's prayers for a child were partly for the wrong reasons. These may have included a fear that her husband Elkanah would divorce her or quite simply, she longed for the taunting from Peninnah to stop. This time, however, she totally yielded her personal ambitions, hopes and dreams for a child to God. Instead, she asked for a child whose life would be completely dedicated for service to God. Hannah's abandonment of her personal desires was key to her breakthrough that day.

Eli was watching Hannah from a distance but he would have been unable to understand what she was saying. So dramatic yet so silent are her prayers but the longer they went on the more Eli was convinced she was drunk and so he interrupted her. Hannah explained what she was doing, '[I] have poured out my soul before the Lord' (1 Samuel 1:15). In other words, she was in fervent prayer before the Lord. All of her suppressed and pent-up emotions were released in those prayers that day. She came to the place where she totally surrendered her deep desire and longing for a baby in exchange for the plans and purposes God had for her life.

After her conversation with Eli, he tells her, 'Go in peace, and the God of Israel grant your petition which you have asked of Him' (1 Samuel 1:17). There was nothing specific in Eli's words to provide confirmation one way or another regarding Hannah's request. Yet her heart is so 'cheered by the priest's comfortable words, and especially by God's spirit setting them home upon her and assuring her that both his and her prayers would be heard, it quickly appeared in her countenance', she was no longer sad (Wesley: In Schoenhals, 1990, p. 180).

Eli's words may seem insignificant to the onlooker but having come through such turmoil, peace in her heart and mind was exactly what she needed. There was no doubt, fear or anxiety in her heart over whether it was going to happen or not. Neither did she question its accuracy or ask for further confirmation or clarification. She had complete confidence, acceptance and trust in those words. It was the Lord's intention that Hannah have peace while she waited for her prayers to be answered. At that very moment, the weight and burden of what she had been living under instantly disappeared. In that place of prayer before the Lord, her sense of purpose, identity and role in the future became clear.

This encounter in the place of prayer was life-changing for Hannah and it was visibly noticeable not just in her countenance but also in her actions. Over the coming days and months, while she waited, she held on to that. Hannah chose to believe God had heard her prayer and would answer.

As we prepare to leave Chapter 5, we, too, are challenged on whether we will choose not only to believe but to hold on to the words and promises God has given us. Your situation might seem impossible, somewhat hopeless and even look like it is getting worse. Your heart might seem so broken and crushed that it feels irreparable. It might even have affected your appetite. During these times, your faith will feel like it has been tested and tried to the uttermost limits.

God wants you to know that He is for you and not against you. He wants you to focus on Him during the purifying and refining process and what He is doing in and through your life. Words in the refrain of the song 'The Blessing'[viii] say 'He is for you, He is for you'. Say that over and over and over again to yourself until it begins to sink in.

Hannah's prayers were more earnest and fervent because of her difficult situation. Likewise, your prayers should also be more earnest, fervent and focused on yielding your ambitions and dreams in place of what God has planned for your life. The most powerful prayers are the silent ones when you have no words to pray and you do not know how to pray. God's plans for you are far greater than you could ever imagine or, indeed, what you could ever achieve. He is working on you during the purifying and refining process in the refiner's fire. God wants you to entrust your child to Him and allow Him to work in and through their life, as well as yours.

God is positioning you for the future ahead. During this time, resist the temptation to become bitter, no matter what your situation might look like, what other people might say, or how long the purifying and refining process may last. God is working all things together for *your* good and for *your* prodigal child. Do not lose sight of this and most importantly, do not let the enemy tell you any different.

Chapter 6

Waiting on the fulfilment of the promises

'You will not need to fight in this battle. Position yourselves, stand still and see the salvation of the Lord who is with you'.
(2 Chronicles 20:17)

Waiting on the fulfilment of the promises of God has been one of the hardest things I have had to do as a Christian parent. As mentioned throughout the book, I have tried to understand and make sense of the past, why this has been allowed to happen and what if anything went wrong. Whilst reflecting back has to some extent, been a helpful process, my time has been better spent focusing on the lessons God wanted me to learn in the waiting room of fulfilment.

Many changes can happen in the waiting room of fulfilment, but one thing which does remain consistent is that God has a plan for your life and your prodigal child's. You may not be aware of it nor see the overall picture just yet but you can be assured that God has not abandoned you, your prodigal child or His plan for both of you. He is working everything out for your good and it will happen in His time. It will not be a day early or a day late. Similarly, all of the promises God has given you about what

He will do will come to pass. Attempting to find a shortcut or negotiate your way out of your storm or fiery trial would not be a good use of your time and energy! Neither is it the time to despise and resent where you find yourself in the plan and purposes of God. Your role during the waiting time is to believe what God has said, trust in Him, be obedient to what He is asking you to do, and wait for Him to fulfil it. Believing matters!

Waiting in general, is not a strength many people possess or do particularly well. Time spent in the waiting room of fulfilment feels like a wilderness, a period of silence. An apparent lack of action during that waiting season makes it tempting to take matters into your own hands and try to provoke or kickstart a change that will force your situation to turn around. The barren feelings that a wilderness can bring make it seem impossible, with the natural eye, for your situation to ever change. If that is where you feel you are just now and the enemy is taunting you about it, be encouraged by the lyrics in this song. 'You are able, Great and mighty God, You are able, Jesus. There is nothing, Nothing you cannot do, Nothing you cannot change, Nothing you cannot turn around'.[ix]

This chapter focuses on some of the lessons I have learned during the waiting season. Because of that, the format is possibly very different from other books that have been written about waiting on God. One key lesson I have learned is about waiting in hope and anticipation for God's promises to be fulfilled. Another was about learning to give thanks in my storm, fiery trial and during the waiting season. This may feel like an oxymoron or contradictory suggestion given everything that has happened and what you are currently going through. If it feels hard or should you not know what to give thanks for, simply begin to 'Thank Him that He takes us to a place where His strength, healing, and power are manifested' in our lives (Conlon, 2018, p. 245).

Hearing His voice in the silence

Waiting can sometimes mean silence. And although we know God has spoken through His word and given us promises relating to our situation and our prodigal child, the results do not happen quickly enough to sat-

Waiting on the fulfilment of the promises

isfy our impatience or timescales. During that period of silence, there are many voices, words and scenarios that spin around inside your head. Do not be fooled and consider that everything which does enter your head is all of God because that would simply not be correct. The voice that says God is not working or that He does not have everything under control can seem very loud during the waiting time. So too, can be the voices that tell you that the situation is so impossible or things have gone so far, they could never be turned around.

Voices and words like that bring anxiety, a fear of the future and a renewed urgency to try to bring about some kind of change. Other voices may try to whisper in your ear that the intensity of this storm, fiery trial and the waiting season is too great for you to cope with, so there is no point in even trying to or indeed continuing any further. So, giving up or walking away is your only available option.

Cutting through all those voices, shutting out the noise and various distractions to allow yourself to hear the true voice of God and what He is saying to you will happen as you spend time reading your Bible and praying. Ask the Holy Spirit to help you hear His voice every day and not miss what He is saying. Not only is the Bible God's personal word and voice, but it is also a secure lifeline for you in your daily walk with God, and it will direct your every step.

You may be asking God how long this storm or fiery trial will go on. Or you might be asking Him what He is trying to say to you in it all. Everything you need to know or want answers to is in His word. The more of God's word you put into your mind, the more you will hear what He is saying specifically to your heart about your situation. God will never lead you in a way that does not line up with His word. He is very precise and specific about what He wants you to do in your life and walk with Him.

God will speak to you about things that are relevant to your personal situation and circumstances. Although the particulars of these are not directly mentioned in the Bible, God will still speak to you about them through the lives of others. Through that, He will give you direction, encourage you, build your faith and draw you closer to Himself as you spend time reading His word and praying. 'The more you hear God's voice in His word, the more you will recognise the voice of His Spirit speaking to you as you pray for His leading' (Omartian, 2012, p. 64).

One of the beauties of the waiting season, and the time spent there, is that it facilitates opportunities for silence and for God to speak because He has your attention. It is not a place where God abandons you and expects you to navigate your way through it alone. Rather, it is a place where we 'begin to live by the promises of God and not by our own circumstances' (Conlon, 2018, p. 243).

Entering that period of silence brings a greater hunger to hear the voice of God not just more clearly but more regularly. Once you begin to hear the Holy Spirit speaking to you through the Bible and other means, that longing for His voice will cause you to look for something every day and you will become dependent on it. Position yourself in prayer and ask the Holy Spirit, 'What do you want to say to me today regarding my situation?' Then you will begin to hear His voice in your ear, leading and guiding you each step of the way during the waiting season.

Living by faith during the waiting season is one of the most difficult things for a Christian to do. We would rather live by sight and use that as a platform from which to put our trust in the promises of God. Having faith while waiting on the fulfilment of the promises involves trusting them even when everything round about you would seem to indicate the contrary and cause you to question or lose hope in them. 1 Corinthians 1 tells us that 'God is faithful [He is reliable, trustworthy and ever true to His promise, He can be depended on]' (vs. 9, AMP). Throughout history, God has demonstrated that He has always kept to His word and has never failed to keep His promises to those who have gone before us. Therefore, God's promises to you are sufficient to keep you going through your waiting season. Turning back or giving up is not an option.

Obedience is the roadmap to breakthrough

The silence and seeming lack of action while waiting on the fulfilment of the promises does not mean God requires *you* to develop a plan or figure out a formula to solve the situation surrounding your prodigal child. The

Waiting on the fulfilment of the promises

promises God has given you will be fulfilled as you walk and follow His leading in complete obedience and yielded-ness. To do that, you must be totally dependent on God to lead, direct and position you where He wants you to be.

As you grow in the Lord and take those tiny steps of obedience, you will learn to become more and more dependent on His leading for your every step. It may not seem like it initially, but there is a blessing in waiting on God's timing. F. B. Meyer put it so eloquently when he said:

'Be still and know that God is within thee and around. In the hush of the soul, the unseen becomes visible and the eternal real. The eye dazzled by the sun cannot detect the beauties of its perihelion [the point in its orbit when a planet or comet is nearest the sun] till it has had time to rid itself of the glare. Let no day pass without its season of silent waiting before God' (In Harvey, 2007, p. 78).

You will be glad that you waited because God does all things well and He works everything out far better than you or I ever could. The Holy Spirit will take that glare away from your eyes and allow you to see more clearly. He will give you those new leads and the light for your next step. It is important to follow His lead carefully and wisely. Obedience is the key to positioning you for the next step God has in His plan and purpose for your life.

Coming aside by yourself to a deserted place and waiting on God is hard. Many find the silence difficult and something to be afraid of, so they often fill it with background noise or sounds. Waiting in the stillness and silence is important to be able to hear what God is saying to you. In the book of Revelation, John, who was referred to as the disciple whom Jesus loved, was exiled to the island of Patmos. John may not have felt particularly loved by Jesus at that time in his life, or indeed like he was having a mountaintop experience. Nonetheless, in the silence and loneliness, John heard a loud voice behind him as that of a trumpet. God used John's exile to Patmos, which despite having magnificent scenery, was a barren, infertile place that lacked inspiration and vitality and was used as a place of banishment and punishment, to speak to John and give him the revelation of Jesus Christ.

Silence in the waiting room of fulfilment can be hard enough to manage. But it is even more challenging to come aside and rest there for a while, particularly when inside, you are screaming for action and change. To rest for a while would signify very little or no action and ultimately no change in your situation. However, in Hebrews 4, we are told that 'a promise remains of entering His rest' (vs. 1).

Matthew Henry's commentary on this passage tells us that 'God has always declared man's rest to be in Him, and His love to be the only real happiness of the soul; and faith in His promises, through His Son, to be the only way of entering that rest'.[9] If we could learn to embrace the silence, be alone with God and rest in Him during our time in the waiting room of fulfilment, it is the secret to spiritual power, blessing, direction and revelation.

Faith is resting in God's love

I have a photo frame on my wall, and below the picture, there is an inscription that reads 'Faith is resting in God's love, knowing He holds the future'. Numerous books, texts and articles over previous years have been written in great depth on the topics of faith and rest in God. While this book does not attempt to discuss either topic in anywhere near the same depth, it has briefly talked about: the meaning of the word faith, growing in faith, walking in faith, unshakeable faith, genuineness of faith, shout of faith, real faith, steps in faith, and building your faith. There are so many descriptions of faith but one of my favourites says it is 'the channel through which all that God has promised becomes ours' (Dunn, 2005, p. 8). When we have faith, we are moved from the blessings we have been promised by God to actually possessing them (Dunn, 2005).

The method to obtain the promises of God has never altered throughout scripture or across time. The principle is still the same. It is 'by faith'.

---

9. https://biblehub.com/commentaries/hebrews/4-1.htm

Eighteen times alone in one chapter of Hebrews, we are told about faith. In fact, verse 6 of Hebrews 11 is clear that 'without faith, it is impossible to please Him [God]'. Although we know that verse of scripture very well, in the intensity of the storm or fiery trial, or indeed in the waiting season, having faith is harder to achieve because of our personal deep emotional pain and sadness.

Being the parent of a prodigal child not only tests the genuineness of your faith but also challenges your willingness and obedience to enter into and remain in the rest God has provided for you during the waiting season. Resting in God's love knowing that He holds the future, should come naturally as a result of having faith in the promises. However, having faith and holding on to the promises during the waiting season may seem a harder ask, especially as there is a lack of evidence, sign(s) of change or even a hint of positive progress. Believing you are in the centre of God's will can also be difficult, especially when your situation appears to be going in the opposite direction to where you think it should. Your faith in the promises therefore fluctuates, and this opens up an opportunity for doubt to creep in. Because of that, finding peace and rest in God's love, in the way He would want you to, is more challenging.

Entering into the rest God has for you begins with making a purposeful choice to have faith and believe in the promises of God. 'Living faith involves trusting the promises of God. Even when everything around us seems to testify to the futility [ineffectiveness] of our lives causing us to lose hope, we are in a covenant relationship with God' (Sproul, 2018, p. 10). D. L. Moody once said, 'There is nothing that can lie in the way of the accomplishment of any of God's promises, but it is conquerable by faith'. You can live by faith and rest in God's love during the waiting season and be confident that He holds the future of your life and your prodigal child's in His hands.

Doubting the promises while waiting on the answer

Receiving a promise from God sounds wonderful and has an illusion that everything from here on is going to be easy, attractive and smooth sailing. When that does not happen, many people doubt the promises and become disillusioned. James Chapter 1 tells us to 'ask in faith, with no doubting for he who doubts is like a wave of the sea driven and tossed by the wind' (vs. 6). The word 'doubting' in this verse means to go back and forth, to be divided in your mind or to debate. It is a divided allegiance or uncertainty as opposed to a fleeting momentary doubt (Nelson, 2018). God wants to accomplish great things through you, but that can only come from a life of faith (Stormie, 2008). There is also no need for you to worry or fear that your faith will fail in the waiting season. Jesus, Himself says that He has prayed for you that your faith would not fail (Luke 22). Neither should you be concerned or doubt that God will keep His promises.

If anyone in the Bible could have doubted and become disillusioned after receiving a word and promise from God, it is Mary, the mother of Jesus. Mary knew the significance of the promise she had been given but also the task which was being asked of her. She is told by the angel Gabriel that the Lord was with her and while these words would have encouraged her, they would also have raised her faith and expectations. Mary does not question how it will all happen but simply responds by saying, 'all generations will call me blessed. For He who is mighty has done great things for me' (Luke 1:48).

After the visitation by the angel, Mary traveled from Nazareth to see her cousin Elizabeth in Hebron. This journey was approximately eighty-one miles on foot. Mary and Elizabeth would have been a great encouragement for each other during the three months they were together. Likewise, Elizabeth would be a comforting presence to Mary. Her years of experience would be an advantage, and she would be a trusted and known person, someone Mary would feel comfortable talking to about the things the angel had said. One of the things they shared in common was the similarly miraculous situations they both found themselves in. Both women were blessed and chosen by God to carry out specific tasks that would require all that head and heart could bring to it. How great it would have been to be part of their conversations!

After this quality time with Elizabeth, we catch up with Mary when she is heavily pregnant. Mary and Joseph have traveled eighty miles from Nazareth to Bethlehem to register for the census. They eventually get shelter in

Waiting on the fulfilment of the promises

the stable and baby Jesus is born. Following the visitation by the shepherds, Joseph takes Mary and baby Jesus and they walk six miles from Bethlehem to Jerusalem to present Him to the Lord and offer a sacrifice. Then as mentioned already in Chapter 2, Mary and Joseph receive a visit from the wise men before hurriedly fleeing to Egypt away from Herod.

Both Mary and Joseph, could be forgiven for doubting the promises of God, feeling disillusioned and indeed questioning the direction they were given for this next phase of their life. None of this was mentioned by the angel Gabriel, and neither was it in the first dream Joseph had. The task of being the earthly parents of God's Son would possibly have seemed a big enough ask without having to travel four hundred and twenty-nine miles [690 km] from Bethlehem to Egypt on foot with a young toddler! It would have been so easy for Mary and Joseph to lose sight of God's promises during this time but instead, they chose to listen to and obey the instructions rather than question them. Although God's plans do not always seem to make sense, we, too, have to trust His purposes without knowing all the circumstances or having the full picture.

Another lesson we can learn from this, and other Bible stories, is that God can speak to you wherever you are and through different methods. He spoke to Mary in the village of Nazareth, a remote corner of the country with no reputation for religion or learning. But He spoke to Zacharias [Elizabeth's husband] in the temple in Jerusalem. The method He used to speak to Mary and Zacharias was through the visible form of an angel, yet He spoke to Joseph in dreams.

I personally love the way God spoke to Samuel in the Old Testament. It says, 'Now the Lord had told Samuel in his ear the day before Saul came' (1 Samuel 9:15). Commentators say God told Samuel privately, by a secret whisper, perhaps a still small voice. The Hebrew phrase is 'He uncovered the ear of Samuel'. Hair is a natural covering, so in other words, God brushed back Samuel's long hair and whispered in his ear. How I long for God to uncover our ears and speak once more to us in that still small voice.

Going back to Mary, I wonder if there were times when she doubted the promises God gave her. Fleeing to Egypt in the middle of the night away from Herod was probably not what she expected as a result of 'having found favor with God'. Neither did the threat to the life of the young child Jesus align with the words the angel told her that He would 'would be great', 'He would be called the Son of the highest', the 'Lord God will give Him the throne of His father David', and that 'He would reign over the house of Jacob forever and of His kingdom, there would be no end'.

In an attempt to answer my own question about whether Mary doubted the promises, I fast-forwarded to John 2, where Mary, Jesus and the disciples were at a wedding. We do not know the full context surrounding the wedding, but it would appear that Jesus and the disciples were invited because of Mary. During the celebrations, Mary comes and tells Jesus that the wedding party has run out of wine. And there, in Mary's instructions to the servants, I found the answer to my question. She simply says, 'whatever He says to you, do it'. Mary had absolute confidence in Jesus, God's Son. She had learned to be obedient and follow whatever step-by-step instructions God gave her, no matter how ridiculous or impossible they might have seemed. The challenges and hurdles she experienced along the way could easily have made her question the accuracy of the promises and caused her to doubt. Yet the Bible tells us she kept all these things and pondered them in her heart.

For God to position and align you for the future, you may have to go through a wilderness experience in the waiting season. The challenging times you encounter there may make you question and doubt the words and promises God has given you personally and those relating to your child. The wilderness can be both a hot and cold place where the strong winds and the lack of cover exposes you to the elements, thus making it an unpleasant experience. Whatever challenges you do encounter, do not doubt, lose sight or deviate from the promises of God while you are waiting for them to be fulfilled.

Yielding to God's way and His timing

Yielding in complete submission to God's way and His timing does not mean you are giving up on your child. You will simply have come to the place where you know and believe with all your heart that God is faithful to perform what He has said He will. Only then will you find that place of rest in God's love and be ready and willing to accept the path and timing He has for you and your prodigal child. Hebrews 4 in The Passion Translation says, 'Now the promise of entering into God's rest is still for us today. So, we must be extremely careful to ensure that we all embrace the fullness of that promise and not fail to experience it. For we have heard the good news of deliverance just as they did, yet they did not join their faith with the word. Instead, what they heard did not affect them deeply, for they doubted. For those of us who believe, faith activates the promise and we experience the realm of confident rest!'

The yielding process is a relinquishing of your own abilities to bring about change within your idealistic timescales and strategies and handing it all over for God to do it in His way and timeframe. Total relinquishment means you are completely reliant and live by every word and promise God has given you. Deuteronomy 8 talks about a man not living by bread alone but by every word that proceeds from the mouth of the Lord. In the waiting season, that might seem hard at first but remember it is a transitioning process that will take time. It has been said copious times throughout this book God has promised that He is working all things together for your good.

Relying on God for your future and that of your child may not come easily or naturally. No one said it would be easy as a parent to place and entrust your child into God's hands. What we do know is that God has proved Himself to be faithful time and time again to others who have done so. And there is no reason or evidence to suggest that anything has changed. Now is the time for you to accept God's word by faith and follow confidently in His footsteps (Conlon, 2018). Taking that first tiny step in obedience will help your faith to grow and then the next step will suddenly light up and become clear.

Proverbs 3 tells us to 'Trust in the Lord with all your heart, and lean not on your own understanding; In all your ways acknowledge Him, and He shall direct your paths' (vs. 5-6). We can see from the stories in the Bible that God has always been more willing to guide His people than they were to be guided, and this scripture is only one example. Just as

God desired to lead and guide those who have gone before, He also longs to lead and guide you in every aspect of your life.

Fear will undoubtedly try to intimidate you during the waiting season but living by faith will help you overcome any unbelief that may try to find a home in your heart and mind. As you draw close to the Holy Spirit and ask Him to take those fears and doubts, He will do it. He will silence the fears with His word. Yielding to God will help transition you from doubt and unbelief to realising there is nothing impossible for God. As it says in Mark 9, 'If thou canst believe, all things are possible to him that believeth' (vs. 23, KJV).

Becoming disorientated and disillusioned in the waiting season is an easy trap to fall into because it does not look nor feel as though you are in the right place or even heading in the right direction. Your inherent natural instinct about what the right or wrong path should feel like conflicts with the path God is leading you on. Should you feel like you are in the wrong place during the waiting season, be careful not to seek an alternative path or course of action which is contrary to God's plans (Carothers, 2012). Worse still, do not try to take matters into your own hands. You must trust what God has told you to do and follow His leading step-by-step through the waiting season. There will be times when the waiting season will seem too long and too difficult to believe God is still there and is going to bring you through it victoriously. Although you may not start out with the kind of faith needed to believe that He can, your faith will grow with each step of obedience you take.

Crazy as it may sound, try to make the most of your time in the waiting season. Just as the eagle uses the winds and updrafts from the hills and mountains, similarly, you can take advantage of every opportunity the waiting season presents and use it with wisdom and diligence (Ephesians 5). Ask the Holy Spirit to open your ears and allow you to hear what He is saying. The amazing work God does in and through your life will be a testimony and encouragement to others who are going through a similar situation.

No tear is wasted

Some commentators suggest David in the Bible was about fifteen years old when Samuel anointed him. Others say he was about twenty. Regardless of what age he actually was, David was, at this relatively young age, a skilful musician, a worshiper, a prolific writer, a great warrior, someone of great strength of character, courage, stability, focus, secure in himself, successful and he had an amazing relationship with Almighty God. After some years had passed, we read in Psalm 142 about his experiences in the cave of Adullam and how he felt during that particular time of his life. David says:

> *'I cried unto the Lord with my voice; with my voice unto the Lord did I make my supplication. I poured out my complaint before Him; I shewed before Him my trouble. When my spirit was overwhelmed within me, then Thou knewest my path. In the way wherein I walked have they privily laid a snare for me. I looked on my right hand and beheld, but there was no man that would know me: refuge failed me; no man cared for my soul. I cried unto Thee, O Lord: I said, Thou art my refuge and my portion in the land of the living. Attend unto my cry; for I am brought very low: deliver me from my persecutors; for they are stronger than I. Bring my soul out of prison, that I may praise Thy name: the righteous shall compass me about; for Thou shalt deal bountifully with me'* (vs. 1-7, KJV).

David was in deep distress. It was a great disgrace for such a great soldier to have to move around so much to ensure his own safety. To be so hotly pursued must have brought great terror by day and night, especially given the continuous threat to his existence. Being constantly on the move would be a challenging enough task, but manoeuvring and hiding four hundred men and possibly women and children as well would have been no easy task.

We are told in 1 Samuel 23 that Saul sought David every day. Saul laid aside all other business and devoted himself wholly to the pursuit of David. This was a time in David's life when he felt he was totally alone. Although David began to doubt whether God was truly for him, he had the presence of mind to pray. Verse 1 of Psalm 142 says, 'I cried out'. Notice the significant emphasis on the vocal and desperate nature of David's cry. One commentator says he cried out with the voice of his mind because he dared not to have spoken with an audible voice in the cave; otherwise, Saul would have heard and thus found him.

Can you picture David in the cave of Adullam and sense the great distress he was experiencing? I imagine the words of David's prayer would have been something like: 'God is this what you called me for? You sent Samuel to anoint me to be king over Israel. I did not ask for this. I was happy tending my father's sheep in the field. Your hand and your call are supposed to be on my life, but here I am in a cave running and hiding for my life. Now I have all these people to look after and feed. I have had to take my elderly parents and find refuge for them and I cannot find refuge for myself. I have done nothing but good for king Saul. Even when he threw a javelin at me, I did not retaliate. Why does he not like me? What have I done to make him hate me so bitterly? Show me what I have done wrong. I will apologise. What do you want me to do? Help me, please.

The cave of Adullam was intended to be a place of refuge, but it had become a place of confinement, namely a prison for David. The word 'overwhelmed' in Psalm 142:3 means in a dark place, closed in. David was in a damp cave. Here as David kneels before God, he is a broken man, crying, prostrate before God. He cannot be vocal about his concerns. He has to keep it all inside while it plays round and round in his head. God has got David alone.

Maybe you find yourself in a similar situation and you are crying out to God and saying, 'Why is this happening to me and my family? I prayed about the path I should take, and I sought your face with my whole heart. I thought I was in your will. Did I get it wrong? What happened? Am I out of your will?

Being anointed of God does not make you immune from storms, fiery trials, or the waiting season. David was in the will of God, but it was his relationship with God that was the key to his success. He knew how to worship, but God taught him how to pray in a cave. God was fashioning David to be the vessel He wanted him to be, and He is doing the

Waiting on the fulfilment of the promises

same with you. I read a quote by Smith Wigglesworth which says 'Great faith is the product of great fights. Great testimonies are the outcome of great tests. Great triumphs can only come out of great trials'. When God leads you to the waiting room of fulfilment, it can be to re-route your life. It is not intended to end it or leave you feeling abandoned.

The title of Psalm 142 is 'A Contemplation of David'. 'Contemplation' in the Hebrew means 'Maschil' or 'a Psalm of instruction'. David called it that because of the good lessons he learned in the cave of Adullam on his knees. He was not ashamed to tell of the frightening situation he found himself in. Neither did he see it as a weakness to cry out to God during those days. Notice that God did not take David out of his situation. He took him through it. David took comfort from knowing God was with Him and knew his case. He expected God would hear and deliver him, which of course, He did. Likewise, God knows how to bring you through your darkest days. David's key to getting through the dark place he found himself in was tears, prayer and praise.

There are references in books and by commentators to the custom surrounding tears. The opening of ancient tombs has uncovered large numbers of tear bottles made of thin glass or pottery bottles. 'They were all made with a slender body, broad at the base with a funnel-shaped top. Every member of the family owned a tear bottle and they collected the tears of the whole family. When serious trouble or death occurred in the home, all the relatives came and each one brought his tear bottle with him. As they wept and wailed, the tears rolling down their cheek, each person took his or her tear bottle and gathered tears from the faces of all present. This bottle was exceedingly sacred to them. It represented all the heartaches, sorrows and bereavements from the grandparents down to the small child. When a person died, his tear bottle was buried with him, as one of his most sacred possessions' (Bowen, 1944, p. 24).

In Psalm 56, David prays, 'Put my tears into Your bottle; Are they not in Your book?' The same verse in The Passion Translation says, 'You've stored my many tears in your bottle, not one will be lost' (vs. 8). God sees the tears you have cried in secret. He has heard your prayers. Praying may not seem like the answer but in prayer, we kneel before God that we may stand before the world and everything that it may throw at us. In prayer, we enter heaven so that we may face the battles on earth. Prayer is the offering up of our desires but also our resignation to God. Prayer is never out of season but is especially seasonable in difficult times. 'A troubled soul finds most ease when it is alone with God who understands the broken language of sighs and groans'.[10]

Are you prepared and ready for your prodigal child to return?

I remember being on my knees in prayer one day at the side of my bed and I heard the Holy Spirit whisper in my ear, 'Are you prepared for your prodigal child to return?' My immediate response was 'Yes, Lord', and I got really excited, thinking that the time for my prodigal child to come home was imminent. Having been quite taken aback by the question, I started to meditate afterward on what the Holy Spirit meant by that. Then I realised that if He was asking me that question, the answer must be that I was not prepared and ready. If that was the case, then how should I be preparing myself and getting ready for my prodigal child's return.

As mentioned in Chapters 1 and 3, many of my times in prayer were spent in uncontrollable tears. For a long time, deep, deep groanings in my spirit rather than words were all that would come out. I knew I was pouring my heart out before the Lord and at times interceding. I also knew that He understood my turmoil and pitiful attempts to tell Him my innermost thoughts and fears. The Holy Spirit started to show me the life and the power of His written word, the Bible. One word from Him was enough to reach down inside, heal the pain and heartache and remove the grief I was carrying. His word secured and stabilised me each day, gave me an anchor, a foundation, hope for the future and provided light for my next step. And so, I believe the first part of my preparation process was to spend time in God's word and allow Him to do a work deep within me.

---

10. https://cocgrey.com/lessons-from-christs-prayer-in-the-garden-of-gethsemane/

Waiting on the fulfilment of the promises

Waiting on your prodigal child to return is not easy. There were days when I felt unable to continue on the path God was leading me on because it seemed like too big of an ask. Fear, anxiety and grief weighed heavy on my heart and rising above them was like climbing a mountain. Looking around at other Christians in similar circumstances as part of some kind of benchmarking process did not help me either because they seemed to have either given up or come through their storm, fiery trial or waiting season effortlessly and victoriously. How easy it was to arrive at the false assumption that we were the only family going through this type of experience.

Finding the strength and courage to take the next step and move in the fullness of the plan and purposes of God for my life felt heavier and harder than normal. As I spoke to the Lord about the weight I felt, He showed me that 'the fears of the sheep are not relieved by the absence of danger but by the presence of the shepherd' (Sexton, 2001, p. 52). He also showed me that it was not His desire that I should be carrying this burden or trying to fight this battle because they both belonged to Him. This was harder for me to accept than at other times because, as a parent, I felt it was my responsibility.

No one else on earth [apart from my husband] loves my child the way I do as a parent, and no one else will stand in the gap on their behalf and fight for them in the same way. I felt it was my 'duty before God to fight for the souls for whom Christ died. Just as some must preach to them the good news of their redemption, just so others must fight back the powers of darkness on their behalf' (Harvey, 2007, p. 108). Relinquishing that responsibility would, in my head transpire into feelings of abandoning my child to an unknown future and I would not be taking the ownership I needed to as a parent.

Many days and weeks went by and it looked like my situation was not changing for the better, nor ever likely to. During the time I spent in prayer, pouring out my heart before God and waiting, the Holy Spirit showed me that my desire for my prodigal child to return had to be laid down and had to die before it could come to life again. Giving my children back to the Lord in prayer is something I have always done and am comfortable with doing. However, laying down my desire for my prodigal child to return was like trying to unearth a very deep root that was wrapped around my heart. Even though I knew I was releasing my child into the hands of Almighty God, laying my desire down and letting go completely was an extremely painful process.

As I did start to release my prodigal child into His care and His hands, He took away the waves of fear, worry, and anxiety and replaced them with His peace which definitely does pass all understanding. During this time, I started to think about Hannah in the Bible and how she must have felt when the day came for her to hand Samuel over to Eli. Handing over your only child in any circumstance would be extremely painful and emotional, but in a strange way, it may have been reassuring if she had known he would be well looked after and raised to be a man of God. Given that Eli's sons were such a negative influence, Hannah must surely have found it even harder to hand Samuel over. Her inability to have any kind of positive influence over Samuel's life once she did hand him over and prevent him from following in the same footsteps as Eli's sons must have left her feeling helpless and hopeless.

Despite not knowing the outcome of her actions, in faithful obedience, she handed over the most precious thing she had to God. In return, not only did God give her the strength to hand him back [to God], He blessed her with more children. Hannah's personal sacrifice was underpinned by her faith in God. Furthermore, it resulted in Samuel living a life that was dedicated completely to serving God. His testimony lives on even to this day and it continues to inspire millions of people across the world throughout every generation that has ever lived.

Laying down my desires for my child meant that I, too, had to place my faith completely in God rather than my own abilities. Faith is one of those deceiving and apparently simple words, yet its complexity and the demands it brings can be high, relentless and intense. The beauty of the Bible is that we can learn about faith from the experiences of other parents who have gone before us rather than starting from scratch and wondering how to figure our situation out. Numerous scriptures highlight 'believing' as being the key to receiving what you ask for in prayer (Matthew 21). However simple that may seem, having faith and believing can be very difficult. Doubting comes so much easier. Nonetheless, we need to learn to

Waiting on the fulfilment of the promises

believe that: God means what He says in the scriptures; He is who He says He is, and He will do what He has said He will do. While human nature wants to see the evidence first and then believe, God wants us to believe and have faith in the things we cannot yet see in the natural.

Although I had released my prodigal child to the Lord, I still felt an underlying helplessness to protect my child. Once more, the Holy Spirit started to speak to me through His word and show me examples of another mother in a similar situation. This time He led me to Exodus 2 and the story of Jochebed, who was the mother of Moses. It is likely that Jochebed was heavily pregnant and due to give birth to her third child [Moses] when the king of Egypt commanded that every son born to the Israelites was to be cast into the river. The anxiety and fear of her newborn baby being a boy must have been intense.

After giving birth, Jochebed and her husband Amram observed the baby be a goodly child and 'more than ordinarily beautiful' (Henry, 1992, p. 96). Matthew Henry suggests that his parents noticed a 'lustre in his countenance that was something more than human and was a specimen of the shining of his face afterwards' (1992, p. 96). Henry also comments that Moses' parents were more 'solicitous [attentive] for his preservation because they looked upon this as an indication of some kind purpose of God concerning him' (p. 96).

After such a perilous three months, Jochebed could no longer hide him. Comprehending what exactly went through her head as she wrapped her baby up and put him in the little ark she made him out of bulrushes is hard. The very thoughts of putting your baby in an ark and laying it in the reeds of a river bank without knowing what the future holds must have been terrifying. Was she hoping that someone would find the little ark and that this would be the means of saving her son? Did she worry that another Israelite family would find him, and then the situation would be no different, and the child's life would still be under threat? Alternatively, what if one of the Egyptians found him and carried out the king's orders to drown all male babies in the river Nile?

Nonetheless, Jochebed was obedient and followed what God had put in her heart at that time, which was to release her son and his destiny into the hands of God. It must surely have seemed that she was relinquishing her child to an unknown future, not least because of the dangers of the river and/or the actions of whoever was likely to find him. She would have known that it would not be long before her three-month-old baby would become restless and need to be fed and changed. Although her daughter Miriam was watching the baby from a distance, Jochebed's heart must have been totally broken as she waited at home for news.

As the sequence of God-ordained events unfolded, Pharaoh's daughter found the child and Miriam was able to suggest getting a nurse for him. God gave Jochebed back her baby son, albeit temporarily, and she was able to raise him as a Hebrew rather than an Egyptian. However, the story does not stop there with a nice happy ending. The day came when she had to hand her child over to Pharaoh's daughter, who would then adopt him as her own and give him the new name of Moses [because she drew him out of the water].

A principle we continually fail to see and comprehend is that God has begun to work long before we see the evidence of it. 1 Samuel 16 is a perfect example of this when the Lord says to Samuel, 'For I have provided Myself a king…'. There had already been a preparation period and at the appointed time, the Lord revealed that He had it all under control. Interestingly, neither Hannah nor Jochebed's roles finished on the day they handed over their children to the Lord. The prayers of these two faithful mothers helped sustain both Samuel and Moses throughout these events. Even though both were following the plan and purpose God had for their lives and their children, the depth of their pain must initially have been intense.

Hannah and Jochebed could not have foreseen how their respective situations were all part of God's plan for them and their children. The lesson we must learn from Hannah and Jochebed is that it does not matter what your eyes see in the natural nor what your instincts tell you. You can entrust your child to a God who is faithful to keep them, keep His promises but who also loves you and your family. Similarly, your life and your role did not finish the day your child headed off to the far country, even though you may feel like it did. As with Hannah and Jochebed, your role is to be a faithful parent and ensure that you remain persistent in prayer, have faith and believe in an awesome God. 'In order to increase your faith, read God's word and ask Him to help you learn to believe Him' (Omartian, 2008, p. 303).

Samuel and Moses both went through life-changing experiences as young children, yet we tend not to think about the impact they had on them. What we do know is that God was with them. He blessed them both abundantly and worked everything together for their good. God spoke personally to Samuel as a young child even when he was in such a precarious place, potentially vulnerable and exposed to the wrong company, namely Eli's sons. And we know from scripture that the Lord knew and spoke to Moses face-to-face. In Acts 7, we read that Moses was 'well-pleasing to God' (vs. 20).

Preparing for your prodigal child's return will require you to continually 'Pour out your heart like water before the face of the Lord. Lift your hands toward Him for the life of your young children' (Lamentations 2:19). Covering your child's life in prayer is an important role for parents. Prayer will change your life and your situation, but it may not always happen immediately. Neither will it happen the way you think or want it to. That does not mean you should give up before your breakthrough has come. Giving up should not be on your list of options. You do not have to strive to understand why all this is happening to you nor figure out how it will be resolved. God knows the reason and the purpose for everything that is happening with you and your prodigal child.

One of the hardest parts of the preparation process is about the continual choices you have to make—choices to trust the promises—choices to have faith—choices to believe and keep on believing. However, one of the hardest choices is to be obedient and, at times, wait and take no action. Exodus 14 tells us to 'Stand still and see the salvation of the Lord' (vs. 13). The choices your prodigal child has made are not what you would have chosen for them, but neither were they your choices to make. God has the direction of your life and your child's planned out. Your choice is to give your life to God and allow Him to lead you. Just as God led the Israelites in Exodus 14 and proved Himself to them, so too He will lead you in the way He has planned out for you (Sexton, 2001).

When the day does come for your prodigal child to return, you will have to consider what your reaction is going to be. The prodigal's father in Luke 15 could have chosen to rebuke his youngest son for his actions in the far country, but he did not. He could have questioned him about what he did with his inheritance and how he squandered it, but he chose not to. Instead, we see the father's compassion and how he ran to meet his son. Even though it was considered undignified for an older man to run, that still did not stop the prodigal's father. Neither did he stop to consider what others might think about him. He had been watching and waiting for his son to return for a long time and when that day finally came, he was quick to forgive and welcome him home.

It may not seem like it at times, but there is a guaranteed answering side to your prayers and it will be revealed in due course (Dixon, 1976). You may ask how it is possible to be sure of that. Well, Jeremiah 33 says 'Call unto me, and I will answer thee, and show thee great and mighty things, which thou knowest not' (vs. 3, KJV). God has promised that He will answer you and He will. In the meantime, go to the Lord in prayer. Call upon Him. Sit before Him in His presence and tell Him all the things that are weighing heavy on you. Do what Psalm 55 says and 'Cast your burden on the Lord and He shall sustain you' (vs. 22). He has promised to hear you in your time of trouble.

As you continue to pray and sit in the presence of God, the Holy Spirit will guide and teach you. Ask Him to open the eyes of your understanding so that you can not only see Him but see His hand and power at work in your life. Keep your eyes of faith and expectancy on the Lord for He will definitely answer you. It may not be the answer you want or, indeed, it may not come in the timescale you think it should. What you can be assured of is that God is always on time and nothing can ever make or cause Him to break His word to you.

Ephesians 3:20 in The Passion Translation says, 'Never doubt God's mighty power to work in you and accomplish all this. He will achieve infinitely more than your greatest request, your most unbelievable dream, and exceed your wildest imagination! He will outdo them all, for his miraculous power constantly energizes you'. Glory will be brought to the name of Jesus if you can but only believe. Then you will be able to sing the lyrics to this song.

Waiting on the fulfilment of the promises

'I love your voice
You have led me through the fire
In darkest night, You are close like no other
I've known You as a Father
I've known You as a Friend
And I have lived in the goodness of God

Chorus

All my life You have been faithful
All my life You have been so, so good
With every breath that I am able
Oh I will sing of the goodness of God'.[x]

So, as you will no doubt have gathered by now, the next steps in my preparation process were to lay down my desires for my prodigal child to return, have faith and believe in God. As I obediently followed His leading, He was faithful in continually reassuring me that He was leading me through the storm, fiery trial, the waiting season, and that He knew the way.

Praising God

Scriptures in the Bible tell us to praise God and although it is engrained in us to do so as part of our Christian walk, for some reason, we do not do it to the extent we should. Neglecting to praise God is generally unintentional but if we really knew the power and impact there is in praising God, it would change our thinking and routines. Praising God has been a theme threaded throughout this book. So far, we have mentioned: the shout of praise confusing the enemy, faith being found to praise, praise feeling out of context; a garment of praise; praising no matter what; the sacrifice of praise.

Praising God will not only refresh and renew your spirit, but it will also fill your heart with joy unspeakable and a peace that passes all understanding. Something happens in the spirit realm when we praise God, which may not always be visible to the human eye. We can see an example of this in 2 Chronicles 20. It says, 'Now when they began to sing and to praise, the Lord set ambushes against the people of Ammon, Moab, and Mount Seir, who had come against Judah; and they were defeated' (v. 22).

Praise lifts the heaviness in your heart brought about by storms and fiery trials. It replenishes your spirit while also putting a smile on your face at the same time. It brings your storms, fiery trials and waiting season back into proportion. Praise focuses your eyes on God and you begin to see your situation from a different perspective, namely through the eyes of God. That is particularly timely and necessary because the waiting season can leave you feeling disillusioned, frustrated and worn out.

Satan will try to tell you God is not faithful, or your situation is hopeless and nothing will ever change. He may even try to tell you that you cannot sing in your storm, fiery trial or during the waiting season. Praise will silence those false thoughts. You can praise in your storms, fiery trials and in the waiting season because this battle belongs to the Lord. You can praise Him in faith, expectation and thankfulness that He is faithful to accomplish what He said He would.

Focusing on your storm, fiery trial or what is or is not happening in the waiting season prevents you from being able to see the blessings and ways in which God is working in and through your life and your prodigal child's. Your role is not to try to figure out what is happening, what might happen, or what you want to happen.

The first thing you need to do is make a conscious choice to praise God. Praising God will open your eyes and allow you to see those blessings being pouring out on you despite everything else that is going on. Looking and focusing your eyes higher above your circumstances will help you see God more clearly. Then you will know that 'the Lord your God is bringing you into a good land, a land of brooks of water, of fountains and springs, that flow out of valleys and hills; a land of wheat and barley, of vines and fig trees and pomegranates, a land of live oil and honey; a land in which you will eat bread without scarcity, in which you will lack nothing' (Deuteronomy 8:7-8).

Waiting on the fulfilment of the promises

You can praise Him, knowing in absolute confidence that He will not leave you where you are. He will bring you through this season victoriously. Some of the lyrics in a song by Elevation Worship says, 'You take what the enemy meant for evil, and turn it for good, you turn it for good…. I'm gonna see a victory, I'm gonna see a victory, for the battle belongs to you Lord'.[xi] Boldly declare His promises as you sing the word of God! 'Dance like the weight has been lifted'.[xii]

Praising and worshipping God as He works in and through your situation is another key step in your preparation process. Yes, there will be days when you do not feel like worshipping and you will have to make a choice to intentionally do so and persevere. Choose to worship Him because of who He is and not because of the way you feel or what is going on around you. It will lighten up your path and guide your next step and your future (Omartian, 2008).

So much happens during worship. Your time of personal worship will develop and deepen your relationship with God. You will hear God speak and experience His love as you intentionally worship Him. Suddenly before you realise it, your emotions, attitudes and thought patterns will begin to change. God will pour out His Holy Spirit on you and enable you to receive what He has for you. The empty places in your heart and life will be filled and He will take away your fears and doubts. Gradually, as you worship, you will also realise that God has lifted you above your storm, fiery trial and circumstances (Omartian, 2008). God said it would not happen 'by might, nor by power, but it by My [His] Spirit (Zechariah 4:6). All the work God is doing in you cannot be accomplished or achieved through your own merits. It must take place in the storm, and only He alone can do it in and through you.

Worship is your route through your dark days. Instead of feeling that you are inadequate or unable to continue, be thankful that you do have those feelings because not only are they normal, it is at that time that you will realise how dependent you are on God. You cannot do this in your own strength. God as your Lord and Shepherd, has a plan for you. It is not a sign of weakness or failure to tell God how you feel or ask Him to lead and guide you.

Praising and worshipping God is one of the ways in which God transforms you. It is not only powerful. It is life-changing. Your heart will be changed, and the Holy Spirit will shape you into the person He wants you to be. Getting to the place where you cannot help but praise and worship Him is precisely the stage God wants you at. You are praising and worshipping because of the promises and spoken word God has given you.

It is hard to fathom with our human mind, but praise is going on in heaven day and night. It never stops. We, too, were created to worship and we do not have to wait until the battle or our storm is over. We can sing, praise and worship God now. We do not praise according to our feelings or circumstances. We praise Him according to His greatness. Rather than crying day and night regarding our circumstances, our focus should be on God, His greatness and His faithfulness to us. Just as the song says, He is worthy of all the praise. 'You are worthy of it all, You are worthy of it all, For from You are all things, And to You are all things, You deserve the glory'.[xiii]

How do you get to that place of faith when circumstances and situations are completely out of your control? For me personally, God brought certain songs across my path, which increased my faith and allowed the word of God to sink deep into my heart and mind. Songs such as 'Do it Again',[xiv] with its heartfelt lyrics.

> *'Walking around these walls*
> *I thought by now they'd fall*
> *But You have never failed me yet*
> *Waiting for change to come*
> *Knowing the battle's won*
> *For you have never failed me yet*

Chorus

> *Your promise still stands*
> *Great is Your faithfulness, faithfulness*
> *I'm still in Your hands, This is my confidence*
> *You've never failed me yet*

Waiting on the fulfilment of the promises

I know the night won't last
Your word will come to pass
My heart will sing Your praise again
Jesus you're still enough
Keep me within Your love
My heart will sing your praise again

I've seen You move
You move the mountains
And I believe, I'll see You do it again
You made a way where there was no way
And I believe, I'll see You do it again'.

Through singing those words, I was telling God I believed in Him and was verbally acknowledging and declaring that this night would not last. All of this helped take my eyes off my circumstances and lift them higher towards Almighty God, the lover of my soul, the one and the only person I can put my trust in and who will never ever break His promises to me.

As this chapter closes, let me ask again. Are you prepared and ready for your prodigal child to come home? If you are not sure, maybe it is time to start preparing and make some changes.

As mentioned at the start of this book, there is a time period that elapses between your prodigal child leaving home for the far country and the day they return. During this time, your faith and trust in God and His promises will be challenged beyond measure but you will emerge from it a different person. The journey has been necessary for your spiritual growth and to prepare you for what God has for you next. Even during your darkest days when you feel brokenhearted and abandoned, the Lord is close to you and has never left you.

Another song that the Lord brought to my attention is called "There was Jesus'.[xv] This song was written by Zach Williams during a time of reflection he had over a 20-year period of his life. Zach explains 'I had no idea that God was in the moment, that He was even with me through some of the things I had going on in my life. Looking back now I can see that He had His hand in everything I was doing. He was creating a way and honestly allowing me to live through some of these experiences',[11] Below are the words of the chorus:

> *'In the waiting, in the searching*
> *In the healing and the hurting*
> *Like a blessing buried in the broken pieces*
>
> *Every minute, every moment*
> *Where I've been and where I'm going*
> *Even when I didn't know it or couldn't see it*
> *There was Jesus'.*

In due course, hindsight will show you that your most life-changing experiences came during the darkest of days. You may never have appreciated that God was all you needed during those dark days until you realised, He was all you had. Just like David mentioned earlier in this chapter, you too, will have learned to depend on God and pray heartfelt, honest prayers to Him in a way like never before. You will have learned to worship God in the midst of your storm, fiery trial and during this waiting season of your life.

---

11. https://freeccm.com/2020/06/09/behind-the-song-zach-williams-shares-the-heart-behind-his-song-there-was-jesus-feat-dolly-parton/

Chapter 7

Lessons

'Seek ye first the kingdom of God and His righteousness, and all these things shall be added to you'.
(Matthew 6:33)

I have tried throughout this book to capture and outline the various things God has spoken to me during this season of my life. It may seem strange, therefore, to have a separate chapter just about lessons. However, there are some key lessons that I wanted to highlight on their own and which in a way underpin what has been said so far in previous chapters.

Self-sacrifice

Society today encourages us to think about and prioritise our own personal needs and desires above others. Self-sacrifice is not so familiar or common a term in either our secular or Christian vocabulary. Yet there are numerous scriptures, including one of the ten commandments, which mention it.

One of the greatest and earliest lessons I learned in life from my mum was that if I honoured God and put Him first, He would bless me and help me get through all the other things on my 'to-do' list. I can truly say that time after time, I have proved that principle of self-sacrifice to be true. During some of the busiest periods in my life, when I put Him first, He gave me inspiration and ideas at work or helped me when I was writing assignments for university. He also helped me get through the practical jobs at home, such as ironing or the housework. Somehow, I seemed to do them more quickly. With every step I took in faith and obedience, God gave me the insight and direction for the next one. What an amazing God we serve. He is interested in the most intricate details of our lives, including those things we think He would not be remotely concerned about!

Despite the many years of following my well-established customary practice of putting God first, I have to say that this was tested beyond my wildest expectations while my child was in the far country. In fact, it was one of the hardest things I have had to do. Not I hasten to add because I did not want to. Rather, it seemed and felt more important to me during that time to leave or put on hold all the things I would normally be involved in and focus on my prodigal child.

What made the situation more challenging were the voices of the enemy that tried to infiltrate my mind during this difficult period. One voice would whisper in my ear that I had failed as a parent. Another would say I had no right to continue in the ministries I was involved in. My child had wandered into the far country, so how could I continue to be a role model or a good example of a Christian parent or leader when things had not all worked out for my family. The voices would also try to tell me that somehow, in my walk with God, I had focused too much on the things of God and got it wrong. Therefore, the penalty for that was my child going astray in search of something more fulfilling. It was the law of the harvest, and I was reaping what I had sowed.

The only place I knew to take those voices was to God in prayer on my knees. If any of those things were true, then not only did I need to repent, I needed to know if God still wanted me in the positions I was in. God left me in no doubt. For every counterfeit voice and whisper of satan, God provided a repeated reassurance of the truth. He kept on leading me and showing me the next step. But not only that, He blessed all that I turned my hand to. The truth of the matter was the storm and fiery trials were because I wanted more of God in my life and had been seeking that closer walk with Him. I had also been praying and asking God for change. What we forget is that for change to happen, certain things will be disrupted.

I opened this chapter with one of my favourite scriptures in the Bible—Matthew 6:33. Even though it is a well-known scripture, it is one that is easier to focus purely on the first part of the verse and overlook the second half. Laying down your dreams, ambitions, desires and hopes for yourself and your family, and seeking first the kingdom of God and His leading, in total obedience is an act of self-sacrifice. But the story does not finish there. It is not just about giving everything up with nothing in return. By taking that step of obedience, God has promised that 'all these things shall be added to you'. All what things you may ask. Well, commentators on this particular scripture link it back to verse 32, which says that your Heavenly Father knows the things you have need of for this present life. So, all these things, the things you need, will be added to you in a measure which is best for you. When you ask for great things [including heavenly things], the little things [including earthly things] will be added to you. And, because God has control over all things, He will give you in the appropriate measure and in His time what is best for you.

Let me give you an example. One of the desires of my heart was to go to university when I left school. But for a number of reasons, there was absolutely no way I could go. I laid down that dream and followed the leading of the Lord and the path He set before me. Although several years had passed since leaving school, part of that path included me working at a university for almost three years—an experience that was both fantastic and frustrating at the same time. As I helped Ph.D. students transcribe their interview recordings or type up their thesis, inside, I kept thinking, 'this is what I want to do someday. At that particular time, there was absolutely no chance whatsoever for that to happen.

When I changed jobs and left the university, I seemed to be moving away from my dream. It seemed so far away at times. I felt like this dream had died. Looking back now, I can see that with each step I took in faith to follow the leading of the Lord for my life, He actually brought me right to the very place I needed to be, which would allow me to go to university. He positioned me perfectly, at the right time. He and only He opened the doors for me to study at university, but it was not just any university. It was the very one that I had worked at and had dreamed about going to for so long!

At the start of this book, I mentioned that I had wanted to write a book someday. Not for a single moment did I ever imagine that God would lead me down this path over the last few years in order to position me to do so. Nonetheless, in that self-sacrificing and giving up of the things I wanted, God has given them back to me and more—just like He said He would. He will also keep, protect and fulfil the plans and purposes He has for my family in and through their lives, at the right time, just as He said He would.

Personal breakthrough

One of the key lessons I have learned during this period of my life is that the 'depth of my surrender to God is positioning me to stand in new places' (Vawser, 2021[12]). I do not know, as yet, what all of those new places are or will look like in the days ahead. What I do know is that surrendering to the ways of the Lord and His processes may sound like an easy thing to do but believe me, it is not. Letting go is extremely painful, and the surrender is so personal, deep and costly. It is something that happens in the secret place with God as opposed to a public place or platform. Letting go stems from a place deep within you but also a desire to truly surrender and give everything to God (Vawser, 2021[13]).

Over the last few years, I have learned so much about personal breakthrough. Firstly, it is exactly what it says. It is personal. It is individual and it is unique to you. What your breakthrough looks like and when it comes will be different from someone else's, even though they may be in

---

12. https://lanavawser.com/i-heard-the-lord-say-your-depth-of-surrender-to-me-is-positioning-you-to-stand-in-new-places/
13. Ibid.

a similar situation to you. Having said that, there are still some lessons that can be learned which are common to everyone.

Following God and His processes requires some serious surrender and letting go. Only through that letting go and dying to self, will the way ahead be made for the expansion to come and for new things to be birthed in your life (Vawser, 2021[14]). Hard as it may be to believe, God needs your testimony. The story of your journey and the miraculous things God has done in your life brings glory to Him. Furthermore, Almighty God is moved when His children take that step of faith and obedience in complete surrender to Him. Your storms and fiery trials can be a personal test to see if you will partner with His way and follow in complete obedience to His plans and purposes. The test can and will challenge whether you are willing to follow God in the sequence of events that He has set out for your life or remain stagnant where you are. Knowing where you are in that process, coming to terms with it and recognising what God is doing in your life will help as you seek that long-awaited breakthrough.

Another lesson I learned is that personal breakthrough comes when you stop asking or expecting others to tell you what only God himself can and wants to say to you. Of course, He may use people or books or dreams. He can use anything or anyone to speak to you. And yes, it is also a good feeling when something or someone speaks directly into your situation without you having said a word about it. But there is no greater feeling in the very depth of your being than when you hear directly from God—that still small voice or whisper in your ear. When that happens, you will know and recognise that it was one of those personal encounters with God, the kind which changes everything. It grounds you, stabilises the multitude of anxious thoughts, and provides direction and reassurance.

Some time ago, a situation happened and I was concerned about the potential consequences for my prodigal child. Not having the full details did not help the situation as it allowed my mind to race and go into overdrive. The situation was inflated in my head and my thoughts were spiraling out of control. I remember I was in the kitchen trying to make plum jam, of all things, and keep back the tears at the same time.

---

14. Ibid.

As I stood there, stirring the pot, the Holy Spirit just gently whispered in my ear that nothing would happen to my child that had not already been ordained. It is hard to fully explain what those words meant to me or the calming impact they had. Once more I realised that God was walking with me in this situation. He was not taken by surprise at what had happened. Neither was He watching from afar off. Rather, He was right there with me as I was going through it. Furthermore, He had something to say to me about it. God wants to communicate more with us as His people on the things which concern each of our lives.

Pursuing personal breakthrough during your storms, fiery trials and in the waiting season is not easy. The enemy will try to tell you that God is not, or cannot, work out your situation because it is too far gone or it is too complex. When satan tries to do that, reflect back and remember the battles and trials God has already brought you through. Remember previous personal breakthroughs and victories. Think about the goodness of God during those times and how He turned it round for His glory and worked it all out for good. He had a divine purpose then and He still has one now. Nothing has changed. He was Lord then and He is still Lord now. God is still working all things together for your good.

Days will come and go where you feel like you are stuck in your situation. Many of us would probably handle difficult times better if we were able to see the way ahead and feel even the slightest sense of positive change. If you are to progress through your storms, fiery trials and the waiting season towards your personal breakthrough, how do you do this? Well, one way is to try to understand and recognise even a little of the purpose and plan of what God is doing in and through your life. It will not only help to ease the pain of the situation but it will help move you on. Onerous as it may seem, keeping a note of the scriptures, the words and the promises God has given you and placing a date beside them will help provide that reassurance that God has and is continuing to speak to you. As you look back, you will begin to see the journey that He has been taking you on. Some of the best lessons you will ever learn are through the deepest of suffering. If you can but trust Him completely, it is possible to have an unshakeable assurance that God has a purpose and He can transform something terrible into something good. Try to find comfort in knowing that all your suffering is not in vain and that God has not forsaken you in your situation.

As you journey with the Lord through your storm, fiery trial and the waiting season, He will help you to recognise the time of that particular season. You do not need to worry about trying to figure it all out. Ask Him to show you. As the blessed controller of all things, every storm, fiery trial and the waiting season is measured and controlled for your good (Dillow, 2007). Do not try to take control of what is happening, as this will result in your focus switching from the blessed controller Himself and moving towards your circumstances. It is not about what trials and tribulations you are going through at this time in your life. More importantly, it is about where the Lord is taking you from in your Christian journey and leading you through as part of His plan for you. Not knowing or being able to see clearly where you are heading can be challenging because you do not understand all the things that are happening to you along the way and how they contribute to the overall plan. Charles Spurgeon's advice helps explain it more clearly, 'If you can't see His way past the tears, trust His heart'.[15]

Do not mistake the presence of trouble as meaning that God is absent in your life. Remember, it is not about what you feel or think you see going on. It is about what you know about God and what He has promised He will do. Some people make the mistake of trying to skip the steps or the processes and the learning God has planned for them during their storm, fiery trial or the waiting season. They try to jump from where they are to simply trying to believe and be strong in the things of God. Some may go as far as to start naming and claiming the possible and impossible, expecting God will prevent them from suffering and heartache and just make everything alright overnight. Sometimes He will, but there is a 'kairos' time when things will suddenly come to a head, and it will be the right moment. It will be that divinely appointed time when you will know it is time to believe for the impossible.

One of the most difficult lessons to learn has been that personal breakthrough comes as you learn to rest in the Lord, knowing He has everything

---

15. https://www.goodreads.com/author/quotes/2876959.Charles_Haddon_Spurgeon

in control. The Apostle Peter writing to the Christians in Asia Minor told them to 'rest your hope fully upon… Jesus Christ' (1 Peter 1:13). In practice, this means we must exhibit confidence that God will accomplish all that He has promised He would do. This phrase 'rest your hope' is such a paradox because 'hope is a constant expectation of an unseen reality' (Nelson, 2018, p. 1688). Therefore, by its very nature, it is more challenging to rest your hope on something that you cannot see or determine. Romans 8 tells us that 'Hope that is seen is not hope; for why does one still hope for what he sees? But if we hope for what we do not see, we eagerly wait for it with perseverance' (vs. 24-25). One of the first lessons to learn from this passage, therefore, is that resting your hope feels somewhat strange and unnatural. The second lesson from this scripture is that in and through all this, God is teaching you perseverance.

We have talked in previous chapters about praising and worshipping God and how you may not always feel like it. Rather, your situation brings tears, an apparently justified brokenness and a heart full of sorrow that cries out: nothing is happening; there has been no change; God is not working; my prodigal child is getting worse and is so lost, there is no way back for them. Part of your personal breakthrough will come when you realise that you do not have to wait until the battle is over to praise God. You can shout now. You can praise now. You can worship Him now. It may not make sense but take some encouragement from one of Spurgeon's suggestions, 'Is there nothing to sing about today? Then borrow a song from tomorrow'.[16]

The power of praise and worship is phenomenal. It will take your eyes off your circumstances and put them onto God. Nothing has taken God by surprise. He knows the end from the beginning. Worship Him because of it. He is worthy of it all. Make room in your life to praise and worship God. Partner with Him through this storm, fiery trial and during the waiting season. He is an awesome God, and you will not be disappointed in Him. You are not being called to be a pioneer and lead the way through this dark period in your life. You are being called to follow.

---

16. https://www.inspiringquotes.us/author/2704-charles-spurgeon/about-songs

Praise and worship will begin to open the eyes of your understanding. It will allow you to see that God is training you in the midst of this battle. Not only are you being trained to follow, but you are also being trained to stand firm on the words He has given you and not be shaken or moved from them. Believe it or not, God is preparing you for the future. He is establishing faith within you, developing your character and strengthening your trust in Him. When you feel like you are breaking down, it is those times that God is carrying you, and you are breaking through. As you begin to emerge from this period in your life, you will declare that only God could have done this.

During the rollercoaster of your storm, fiery trial and the waiting season, times will come when you feel you have nothing left to fight with anymore and you may even feel alone in your situation. Use these times to allow God to breathe life into you. You will never be the same. It is not that you have nothing left to fight with. It is a new level of surrender, yielded-ness and abandonment of self, your will, your dreams and your desires. Set aside your weariness, your cares and your anxieties and just worship Him. Be surprised at how He renews, refreshes and enlightens you from the things that have been holding you down.

Regardless of how isolated your situation may seem compared to others around you, rest assured that you are not alone. Neither are you unique in history to encounter trials and tribulations? Spurgeon, in one of his most famous sermons entitled 'Songs in the Night', captured the challenges and praise and worship so precisely. Here is an extract:

> *'Night is one of the greatest blessings men and women enjoy; we have many reasons to thank God for it. Yet night is, to many, a gloomy time.... Night is the time of terror and alarm to most men and women. Yet even night has its songs.*
>
> *Have you ever stood by the seaside at night, and heard the pebbles sing, and the waves chant God's glories? Or have you never risen from your bed, and opened your bedroom window, and listened? Listened to what? Silence—except now and then a murmuring sound, which seems like sweet music.*

> *And have you not imagined that you heard the harp of God playing in heaven? Didn't you conceive, that the distant stars, those eyes of God, looking down on you, were also lips of song—that every star was singing God's glory, singing, as it shone, its mighty Maker, and his lawful, well-deserved praise? Night has its songs.*
>
> *We don't need much poetry in our spirit, to catch the song of the night, and hear the planets and stars as they chant praises which are loud to the heart, though they are silent to the ear—the praises of the mighty God, who holds up the arch of heaven, and moves the stars in their courses.*
>
> *Man, too, like the great world in which he lives, must have his night. For it is true that man is like the world around him; he is a little world; he resembles the world in almost every thing; and if the world has its night, so has man. And we have many a night—nights of sorrow, nights of persecution, nights of doubt, nights of bewilderment, nights of anxiety, nights of oppression, nights of ignorance—nights of all kinds, which press upon our spirits and terrify our souls.*
>
> *But, blessed be God, the Christian can say, 'My God gives me songs in the night'. It's not necessary to prove to you that Christians have nights; for if you are Christians, you will find that you have them, and you will not need any proof, for nights will come quite often enough'.*[17]

God is doing a new thing in you, and the way to where you are going is through the desert. Praise Him as you journey through the season you are in. 'Do not remember the former things, nor consider the things of old. Behold, I will do a new thing. Now it shall spring forth. Shall you not know it?' (Isaiah 43:18-19). It is our wonderful Saviour 'who gives songs in the night, who teaches us more than the beasts on the earth.... You must wait for Him' (Job 35:10-14). Understanding what that new thing is may not initially be easy or apparent, which in turn makes personal breakthroughs more difficult. Appreciating that there is a journey to get from where you are now in the Lord to where He wants you to be

---

17. https://www.biblebb.com/files/spurgeon/2558.htm

will help reassure you that there is a purpose in it all. You do not need to worry about how you are going to get there. Job 23 says, 'But He knows the way that I take; When He has tested me, I shall come forth as gold' (vs. 10).

On dark days, when you have reached breaking point for the umpteenth time, you may question whether you are on this journey alone or how much longer you have to go in this season of your life. Keep it at the forefront of your mind and thoughts that you can trust Him to lead you through. Just as Job said, 'He knows the way that you take'. Should your faith feel like it is on trial, recognise that God is demonstrating His strength through your weakness. Then when your storm, fiery trial or the waiting season is over, you will come out like gold just as He promised you would (Job 23).

The story of Job finishes with a conversation between him and God. Job acknowledges that he has come to a new and deeper relationship with God as a result of his trials. Like Job, while you are going through difficult times, you may not always see the beneficial results from the trials which have been allowed in your life. Often it is only afterward that they start to unfold. In the present, as you go through situations, those storms, fiery trials and the waiting season seem devoid of meaning and will feel contrary to the direction in which you think your life should be going (Bridges, 1993). Regardless, you are commanded to trust God, His word, His promises, and His wisdom. Personal breakthrough comes when you stop trying to work it out yourself. Stop trying to fix it! Save yourself time and needless effort exploring different options to turn your situation around. Simply close your eyes, listen for His voice and humbly follow His leading and His command.

The more I read about God's promises, the more it becomes clear that they are irrevocable. Although they are unconditional, they are underpinned by faithfulness and obedience to God's command that you walk before Him. 'The Lord's unfailing love surrounds the one who trusts in Him' (Psalm 32:10, NIV). His love cannot fail no matter what hardships you go through. He wants you to grow through adversity by reading His word and following His leading. It is not His intention that you perish in adversity.

Ask God to bring relevant passages of scripture, such as Psalm 94, to your attention to help you see how adversity and instruction join together in God's training process. 'Blessed is the man whom You instruct, Oh Lord, And teach out of Your law, That You may give him rest from the days of adversity' (Psalm 94:12). You will benefit from reading these kinds of passages in the Bible and, at the same time, gain new insights into the scriptures and the lives of the respective characters who have gone before you.

Submitting to the sovereignty of God, persevering to co-operate with Him and trusting His wisdom will help you to transition from knowing about God to knowing Him more deeply and personally (Bridges, 1993). You may not understand what God is doing in your adversity nor immediately discover what possible good there could be in the darkness of your storm, fiery trial or the waiting season. But one day you will be able to look back and know that the most beautiful work of your life was undertaken during those days. You will also know that it is possible to be at peace in the midst of the storm and the dark days. God will 'come from a place within where you think that you have no strength' (Roberson, 1999, p. 239).

Persistence in breakthrough

God has called you to do more than endure adversity. He has called you to persevere in spite of it and in the face of it. 'Perseverance is the quality of character that enables one to pursue a goal in spite of obstacles and difficulties' (Bridges, 1993, p. 185). Such obstacles and difficulties can most definitely challenge your perseverance in so many ways, but some of the hardest battles to overcome are those in your mind. The Lord himself was tempted and tested in the wilderness by the voice of satan. Unlike the Lord, we have to recognise the difference between the voice of God and that of the enemy.

Persevering during storms, fiery trials and the waiting season can be hard when it looks like there is no change and nothing is happening. It is at those times that you can be most vulnerable, and the devil will try to whisper in your ear to forget the whole God thing and be done with Him. He has not answered your prayers. Another lie he may try to tell you is that if your child is not going to follow the things of God, then the best you can hope for is that they are a good citizen and do not do anyone any harm. His lies go even further than that. They may try to tell you: it does not matter about your child's soul; God is not real; hell is not what it is made out to be; your child is so far gone there is no point of return; your child has made their decision so let them get on with it, at least you are okay.

Several times throughout this period in my life I have heard satan whisper these types of words in my ear. So much so that they haunted me until I was in complete turmoil inside. Such words gripped my mind and heart so viciously that I had once again to get before the Lord. The devastating thoughts and their potential consequences caused me to fall on my face before the Lord and cry out for mercy for the soul of my child. There was a critical sense of urgency in my head regarding my situation. I needed to talk to God about these words, but I also needed Him to speak to me and tell me about the situation from His perspective. Deep down, I thought God needed to act quickly and restore my prodigal child before it was too late. Yet no matter how much I prayed and earnestly sought His face, the answer and breakthrough did not come.

One of the scriptures God led me to was Matthew 15. It is a beautiful story of a mother who persisted in breakthrough. As I read that passage, it was the phrase 'Have mercy on me' that stood out (vs. 22). There are over fifty different topics relating to mercy in the Bible and it sets the context for many of Jesus' teachings. Mercy is a quality of God and one that He requires of His people, but what does it actually mean? Well, one author describes mercy as 'love that responds to human need in an unexpected or unmerited way'. Mercy causes the impossible to become possible. It surpasses all situations.

I could not understand why the woman in that passage of scripture (Matthew 15) asked for mercy for herself and not for deliverance for her daughter. Surely that was the very reason she came to Jesus. To find some meaning behind her words, we need to understand that she was a Canaanite from the local area. Canaanites were traditionally looked down upon by the Jews as being unworthy of God's blessings because they were not of the house of Israel. So, this woman believed she was culturally unworthy of God's blessing and therefore unable to come to Jesus on the grounds of merit.

The passage does not tell us how or when her child became severely demon-possessed. Neither does it say how the demon possession affected her child, but regardless of that, no parent would want to see their child suffer like this. It would have been easy for the woman to blame God for allowing this to happen to her young child. Yet, for this Canaanite woman, her path may never have crossed with Jesus had the child never become 'demon-possessed'. Her life was worlds apart from His, both geographically and culturally. Despite the hardship of her situation, it was part of God's plan to draw her to Himself.

Whatever turmoil went through her head as she approached Jesus, we do not know. But when she stood there before Jesus, all that came out were the words 'Have mercy on me O Lord Son of David'. This woman's simple request was for mercy. By approaching Jesus, she ran the risk of public ridicule. She was asking for something that others thought she was not entitled to. Her bold, courageous faith to believe that Jesus would show her mercy, heal her daughter and change her situation was incredible. Notice that her faith and dependency on Jesus for this miracle lay entirely upon the words and testimony of others. She did not have previous personal experience of Jesus' miraculous power to draw upon.

Sometimes we try to form a picture in our head about how situations are going to unfold or how God is going to change our circumstances but it does not always work out the way we think it will. That is exactly what happened to this woman. Verse 23 says, 'He answered her not a word'. Look at her words and approach, she cried out to Jesus. The word 'cry' in this passage means turmoil. It is taken from the word 'clamor', which means to shout loudly and insistently, make a passionate, earnest demand. In the Greek text, the word is an imperfect tense which means that it continued for some time. In other words, she stood afar off, repeatedly shouting, 'Have mercy on me O Lord, Have mercy on me O Lord'. Yet despite the repetitive insistent shouting, Jesus still answered her not a word.

This mother had an urgency about her situation, but it was not echoed by Jesus. Indeed, the apparent lack of response seems harsh but the silence did not mean Jesus was not listening. The test for her was about faith and perseverance. It is a beautiful picture. Jesus was there and He heard her but by not answering her immediately, she drew a little closer. Rather than shouting 'Have mercy' from afar, she then came a little closer and began to worship, saying, 'Lord help me'. Again, this is an imperfect tense in the Greek text and so she repeated it over and over.

Her story shows the strength of her faith and persistence to break through for her child. More importantly, her faith and persistence pleased Jesus. There is no doubt that the lack of an answer in your own life can be discouraging, almost paralyzing, particularly when you have earnestly cried out to God yet there is no response and no change seems to be taking place. The temptation to turn away, assuming Jesus is not interested or is not listening, is extremely high. Psalm 94:19 describes some of the turmoil that can go on in your head when you feel God has not heard your prayers, but it also tells us how Jesus comforts us during those times.

> 'In the multitude of my thoughts within me, which are noisy like a multitude, crowding and jostling one another like a multitude, and very unruly and ungovernable, in the multitude of my sorrowful, solicitous, timorous thoughts, thy comforts delight my soul; and they are never more delightful than when they come in so seasonably to silence my unquiet thoughts and keep my mind easy'.[18]

Had the woman in this passage yielded to the temptation to turn away or listen to the turmoil going on in her head, she would have missed out on her daughter being healed. Thankfully she did not make that decision and we then read that although she started off calling Jesus 'Son of David', it then became personal and she ended up calling Him 'Lord'.

God knows how to get your attention. He sees the tears you have cried in secret. He has heard your prayers. He is there even though it feels

---

18. https://www.biblestudytools.com/commentaries/matthew-henry-complete/psalms/94.html

like He is not, or when it seems that He is silent on the matter. Your sense of urgency does not always align with God's plan and purposes for your life and your prodigal child's. Continue to persevere and breakthrough for your prodigal child. He is listening and He will answer. God wants you to draw a little closer.

The 'weight of the wait'

The waiting time from when your prodigal child goes into the far country until they return will vary for every family. For some, it can span many years. As the days, weeks, months and even years pass by, you can feel spiritually, emotionally and physically shattered. Not long after one storm or fiery trial has passed, along comes another one to take its place. Being the parent of a prodigal child can also feel lonely and it is easy to forget that other parents across the world today have or are currently experiencing similar situations and feelings to you. Nonetheless, at times there seems to be nothing but disappointment after disappointment for many parents of prodigal children. For others, there may well be glimmers of hope along the way that their prodigal child is or has turned a corner and is on their way home, only to be disappointed again.

All these experiences add up, and on occasions, they feel like a heavy weight that can be felt physically in your body. Throughout this book, I have encouraged you to try and understand what God is doing in and through your situation. As well as that, it is also necessary to try to understand and recognise what is going on in your physical body and why you may feel so heavy and emotionally and spiritually downcast. Ana Werner, in one of her Facebook posts, calls it the 'weight of the wait' (September 2021[19]). She challenges readers to consider whether they can handle the 'weight of the wait'. Each one of us likes to think we can handle whatever comes our way, but that is not always the case. Ana reminds us that no one escapes the call to wait and challenges us to rethink how we view the waiting time.

---

19. https://www.facebook.com/anawernerministries

Lessons

'We often look at wait seasons as times of setbacks but they really are seasons of preparation. It's a time of growth and change. It's in the waiting where we are transformed' (Werner, 2021[20]).

Without a doubt, it can be hard to understand the reason and purpose for storms and fiery trials. John Charles Ryle, an English Evangelical Anglican Bishop, described trials as 'an instrument by which our Father in Heaven makes Christians more holy. Trials are intended to make us think, to wean us from the world, to send us to the Bible, to drive us to our knees'.[21] Finding some insight and understanding of what God is doing in your life will help you move towards your personal breakthrough. You will also be able to find some rest in the waiting room of fulfilment—but not just any waiting room—God's waiting room.

It is not God's intention that you should buckle under the weight of adversity nor the 'weight of the wait'. When that weight starts to feel heavy, recognise it for what it is and give it back to the Lord. You do not have to carry that heavy load. Matthew 11 tells us, 'Come to Me, all you who labour and are heavily laden, and I will give you rest. Take My yoke upon you and learn from Me, for I am gentle and lowly in heart and you will find rest for your souls' (vs. 28-29). The battle is not yours, it is the Lord's and you do not need to try to bear the weight of it. Neither do you have to try to figure it all out.

God does not mean you to just survive your storm, fiery trial or the waiting season. He has got everything under His control and He wants you to grow and thrive through it. However, there are some key lessons you should be aware of. Firstly, there are no shortcuts. Neither is it possible to push your way to the front of the queue for answers! Secondly, it is possible to have peace during the waiting time. Thirdly, you will gain the most benefit from your storm, fiery trial and the waiting room experience when you allow God the opportunity to change and transform you through it all. Fourthly, as you wait, be blessed as you watch God moving on your behalf and working all things together for your good and

---

20. Ibid.
21. https://gracegems.org/30/short_pithy_gems_from_jc_ryle.htm

for your family, just as He said He would. Fifthly, recognise that this is God's doing. Sixthly, take courage, knowing that with man, it would be completely impossible to turn things around, but not with God.

Finally, waiting for a breakthrough to come can definitely be hard and draining. It is important to recognise that there is an enemy who will try to bring division in families and homes through the simplest and silliest of things. Do not take the bait of the enemy on these when they arise. This is the time to draw close to the Lord and create time and space for God to speak. There is a letting go during the waiting time, a shift that is taking place and it is most definitely a change of pace. It may feel like time has stopped, and priorities are shifting. Letting go and dying to some things should not be confused with giving up and feeling like you have lost the battle. These things are necessary to make way for God to do what He is going to do.

God is in the business of uniting families, healing hurts and building back better than before. If we try to hold on to the old, we will not be able to grasp the new. It is time to sing a new song of victory! 'There is a song. I know it well. A melody that's never failed. On mountains high, in valleys low. My soul will rest, my confidence, in You alone. Hope has a name. His name is Jesus. My Saviour's cross has set this sinner free. Hope has a name. His name is Jesus. Oh Christ be praised, I have victory' (Hope has a name, River Valley Worship[xvi]).

Compassionate Saviour

Many times, we have heard people saying that God is interested in families. In my experience, 'interested' is too shallow a word to describe the extent God goes to and His attention to the most intricate details in your life and your family's. He is a loving, compassionate Saviour. You do not have to look far in the Bible to find an example either of where someone has gone to Jesus about a member of their family or household or where Jesus has sought a family out.

One such example is in Luke's gospel. In the first few verses of Chapter 7, Jesus had been at Capernaum, which was an important town on the northwest shore of the Sea of Galilee. It was a town whose economy was centred on fishing and agriculture. Luke tells us that a certain centurion's servant was sick and ready to die. When the centurion hears Jesus is in town, he sees an opportunity for his servant to be healed. Being a gentile himself, the centurion may well have thought Jesus would not care to converse with someone like him. So, he comes up with a plan and instead of going to see Jesus himself, he decides to send some Jews. Not just any Jew, he sends elders of the Jews. These were men not only advanced in years, but they were also of a distinct social class and considered to be 'the wise'.

The story does not tell us exactly what message the centurion gave to the elders of the Jews. But for some reason, they [the elders of the Jews] seemed to feel the message and request for healing needed to be 'beefed up' a little and justified. The simple facts of the story were that the centurion's servant is sick, he is going to die, can Jesus come and heal him.

Although the elders do give Jesus the message and the facts, they throw in their own additional thoughts and say that the servant should be healed because the centurion loved the nation, he built them a synagogue and he paid for it out of his own pocket. Maybe the elders thought that a case based on good deeds and merit would be enough to convince the Master to heal the servant!

On the day after the centurion's servant was healed, Jesus and His disciples then travelled from Capernaum to the city of Nain which lay at the base of Mount Moreh between Endor and Shunem. The word Nain means beauty, pleasantness, and green pastures. However, this particular story tells of the sadness, tragedy and frailty of human life. It is a story that is all too familiar even in the days in which we live. The story seems somehow to be even more sorrowful when we read in verse 12 that the young man was 'the only son of his mother and she was a widow'.

In Bible days, funerals were normally held on the day of death because keeping a body overnight would mean the house would be unclean. Indeed, contact with a dead body was viewed as the severest form of impurity. Everything about funerals moved so fast that it left no time or space to come to terms with what had happened.

There were other certain customs that had to be adhered to. Firstly, the burial place had to be outside a community, and the widowed woman was required to lead the funeral procession through the streets and out of the city gates. Relatives and neighbours would surround her, trying to support her as best they knew how. Other members of the community who heard a funeral procession going by would normally join it from behind.

The funeral procession would also have a band of professional mourners with their flutes and cymbals. Nothing about this funeral procession was quiet, especially with the noise of the professional mourners, the instruments, the crowd, the noise of city life, the passers-by. We know from the story that the widow herself was visibly weeping aloud and distressed, her grief being understandably immense. The noise, combined with the sheer emotion and sadness of the situation, would have made this a very difficult and almost unbearable procession.

This woman is referred to and known in the gospels as the 'widow of Nain'. That is correct because that is what she was. But she was also a mother who had suffered a double tragedy of losing her husband and now her only son—a mother going through the motions. A mother swept along by the funeral customs and rituals of the day, which had to be performed. There is such an unfairness about the situation this woman finds herself in. She possibly married, thinking she and her husband would grow old together, and as parents, they would see their child(ren) and grandchildren growing up. In reality, somehow, the normal cycle of life was mixed up and out of sequence and she finds herself having to bury her only son.

Let us consider this story for a minute from the widow's perspective. In a town the size of Nain, it would not have been unusual for passers-by to stop and pay their respects as the funeral procession passed through. Here she is with her friends, possibly extended family and her neighbours on one of the most difficult days of her life. She has led the procession through the streets, as was the custom. And as they journeyed through the city gates, a stranger approached her, not from behind but in front of her. I do not think for a minute that Jesus would have shouted from afar at the woman. I believe He would have walked up and stood close to her, observing her intently. He would have seen her tear-stained face—a face that spoke of sadness, heartache, hopelessness and despair. A mother weary with the weight and rollercoaster of emotions as they ran through her head and heart—a mother whose heart was totally broken and aching.

Verse 13 says, 'when the Lord saw her, He had compassion on her'. The word compassion means to feel deep emotions—to have sympathy—and understanding of her situation, to have empathy—to be able to identify with how she feels. Luke tells us about the compassion of the Saviour and that He was moved to the depths of his heart for this woman. There is no stronger word in the Greek language for sympathy. We are not told what Jesus' actions were. Maybe He reached out and took her by the hand or by the arm to catch her attention. Or maybe He cupped her face in His hands and lifted up her head so that she looked at Him. No matter how He caught her attention, as He looked at her, He saw her eyes filled with tears. Eyes that once sparkled with love, laughter and life were now sad, dull and empty. He was moved by her situation. He had compassion on her.

As she looked back at this stranger—His eyes—oh, those beautiful eyes had such tenderness, care and compassion. So full of love and life. He was like no other human being she had ever encountered. As this stranger looked at her, He said three words over and over 'Do not weep, do not weep'. Oh, why did He keep repeating the same words? She heard Him the first time and the second. Why did He keep repeating them? To the onlooker, this stranger would have come across as someone trying to console a woman who was so heartbroken that she simply could not be consoled. The repetition of words may even have come across as unkind, unreasonable and unsympathetic. Given her situation, how could anyone expect this widow woman, this mother, not to feel emotions? How could anyone possibly request her not to weep?

Jesus knew the depth of this mother's tears. She had already lost her husband and now her son's death had broken and shattered her dreams and hopes for the future. Loneliness would take the place of the family unit, friendship and companionship. Beneath the tears and sadness, Jesus saw something else. He saw her fear of what the future would hold, a fear of the unknown. Her son's death would mean the end of any comforts she had known because women in Bible days would not be able to earn an adequate income to sustain themselves. Now the person on whom she was depending upon to look after her in her old age was gone. It is said that fear can affect us in a similar way to the multisensory experience we get during weather storms.

We can feel fear in the pit of our stomach, in the clamminess of our hands. We hear the fear in the negative things we say. We can feel fear as a situation plays out either in our minds or in reality. All those senses of fear can paralyse and immobilise us. Fear can grip us when we think that something undesirable is going to happen and no matter how hard we try or what we do, we cannot stop its course. Fear can get a hold of our lives and start to dominate or demoralize us. Sometimes our fears are logical, sometimes illogical. Fear can show as anxiety, nervousness, worry, stress, dread, and tension. It eats away at our lives and our self-confidence. Fear impacts our mental and physical health and our rational thinking. It taunts us, robs us of sleep and rest and threatens to haunt us for the rest of our lives.

In the midst of the sadness of this story, there is something beautiful. As the funeral procession comes out of the city gates, no one anticipated that they were on a collision course whereby death and sadness would meet life and joy head-on. Look at the precision in timing and sequence of events. It was not a coincidence that Jesus just so happened to be arriving at the city gates at the same time as the funeral procession was coming through. God is never too early and He is never too late. His timing is absolutely perfect. He is absolute perfection.

As we come to the end of Chapter 7, there are such contrasts between the story of the centurion's servant and the widow of Nain. The centurion sends a request for healing and he has the faith to believe in it. The widow of Nain did not ask for a thing. Yet the lives of both families were changed and transformed by the spoken word of the Master. We do not know much about the centurion's servant or the widow's son—whether they had been ill for a long or short time. We do know that the widow's son was a 'young man'.

Jesus went over and touched the open coffin and those who carried it stood still. Imagine what was going on in the minds of the pall-bearers. From their perspectives, this stranger wants to pay his respects and speak to a young man who has passed on into eternity. It must have seemed absurd, ridiculous even insensitive to the onlooker. To the best of their knowledge, He did not know the widow's son, nor did He have any connections with the family. What could this man called Jesus possibly want to say? Besides, what good was it going to do anyway? Did He not think the widow had suffered enough?

The words of Jesus were simply, 'Young man, I say to you, arise'. 'Arise' means to get up, stand up from your position of death, of lifelessness. But this was no ordinary command. It was directional and there was power in the spoken word of the Master. A power so strong it was able to put life back into this young man when he had no power or ability of his own to do anything. The command came from the one who holds the keys to death and life. He is the mighty God, a wonderful compassionate Saviour. Christ's power over death was evidenced by the immediate effect of His spoken word. After the young man sat up and began to speak, Jesus gave him back to his mother to attend to her as a dutiful son. The astonishment and fear that rippled through the crowd must have been significant.

This story tells us loud and clear that God is not a cold, distant God. He is a loving, compassionate Father. You can sense His gentleness, the personal interest and understanding He had in this widow woman of Nain. And He has the same interest in you and your family. He wants to turn your life around and that of your prodigal child's. Sometimes like the centurion we invite Jesus to come into our lives, to change things. At other times we do not realise that the difficult times we go through have been allowed to bring us to Jesus. We are on a collision course with a wonderful compassionate Saviour.

Sadly, we have become so focused and almost obsessed with seeing evidence of Jesus working before we will believe or have faith in Him. It dominates and dictates our thoughts and emotions so much so that it can prevent us from moving forward in foggy situations. To help see things differently, allow yourself to digress for a minute and consider nature's growth process. Much of what God is doing in your life and that of your prodigal child's is taking place underground [inside] and you cannot see it. You may look at the ground which appears dry and hard. With the natural eye you are looking for cracks or breakthroughs in the ground that would indicate growth or movement. The absence of any signs of life is discouraging and causes you to lose heart, fall under the weight of weariness and even lose momentum in the things of God.

One of the lessons from the stories of the centurion and the widow of Nain is about having faith in God even when there are no signs of life or change. Regardless of what you see, or think you see, do not lose that expectation of breakthrough which God has promised you. Change will not happen 'by might nor by power but by My Spirit says the Lord of hosts' (Zechariah 4:6).

Hold on to the promises God has given for you and your prodigal child. Keep trusting and have faith, even though it may be as small as a grain of mustard seed. The rumbles of movement and change will start and will get stronger. Breakthrough will come. Satan is terrified of what God is doing in and through your family. He would rather keep you down in disappointment, discouragement and disillusionment. Satan would rather you would throw it all in and stop believing and trusting in God. Remain at peace in the midst of your storm, fiery trial and during the waiting season. God is not a man that He should lie. This is a time to draw close to God and ask Him what He is doing in your family during this season. Stop and take the time to listen. It will be worth it.

Chapter 8

'Dark nights of the soul'

'For God has not given us a spirit of fear, but of power and of love and of a sound mind'.

(2 Timothy 1:7)

Despite the many valuable lessons we learn along the way, fear still has a way of gripping our lives particularly during storms, fiery trials and in the waiting season. Being the parent of a prodigal child is no exception, if anything it can feel somewhat exacerbated. While books have been written about personal fear(s), how to overcome them, how to be fearless, feeling fear, or the guilt of fear, less has been written about the fears a parent may have regarding their prodigal child.

In previous chapters of this book, there are references to: containing fears; fearing the worst; identifying/defining fears; talking to God about your fears; giant of fear; faith being the antidote to fear; facing your fears; fearing the fiery trial; being intimidated by fear; the weight of fear; experiencing fear in your physical body. Neither this book, nor this chapter aim to go anywhere remotely near the depths of other writings which focus solely on the topic of fear. It is simply intending to help you recognise some of the feelings of fear that may be going on inside you as the parent of a prodigal child.

Tempting as it may be to think that fear is a new phenomenon to the generation and the times in which we live, we know from the Bible that it has existed since time began. Indeed, the word fear is referenced over 390 times in the Bible. Fear is however, said to be the 'primary and most severe disease' in the 21st century…. it's energy can affect a person's spiritual, physical and psychological health'. In addition to that, its byproducts are said to 'trigger other diseases' (Conlon, 2012, p. 13).

Becoming a parent for the first time may have brought you some initial, yet understandable, and completely natural fears. However, as you settled into your new parental role and gained confidence in how to handle and look after your new baby, those initial fears most likely disappeared. That is of course until the baby started to grow and develop, and those previous fears were replaced with new ones! However, becoming the parent of a prodigal child takes fear to a new dimension and possibly one which you have not previously considered or encountered. Fears surrounding your prodigal child may be dominating your every thought during the day or causing you to lose sleep at night.

Finding purpose and trying to understand what God is doing in your life during such times has been a common theme throughout this book. Some of the lessons you have learned could only have happened during those times which Stormie Omartian refers to as 'dark nights of the soul', otherwise known as those periods in your life when God has your undivided attention and you have nothing but Him to cling to (2008, p. 269). For those of you who do experience this, 'take comfort in the fact that God uses these times of darkness to teach us invaluable lessons we might never learn in the light' (Omartian, 2008, p. 269).

As I write this chapter, it is difficult to put down on paper some of the fears that have entered my head as the parent of a prodigal child. This is partly because they do not deserve a mention or even an acknowledgement given that they are so far removed from the word of God and His promises. However, as you read this chapter, I trust it will help you to recognise the lies that satan may have been trying to infiltrate in your mind, just as he tried to do with me. You cannot prevent thoughts from coming into your head, but you certainly do have a choice as to what you do with them and whether you choose to believe them.

'Dark nights of the soul'

Fears of the heart

One of the biggest fears a Christian parent can have, is that their child will go to a lost eternity [hell]. Not many preachers talk about hell these days because it is uncomfortable to do so. But that does not change the fact that it exists. Jesus himself talked more about hell than He did heaven. He spoke of a time when mankind will be separated into two groups—those who were foolish and unprepared for the bridegroom's return and those who were wise and prepared (Matthew 25). When our time here on earth is over, there are only two places to go. Either we will spend eternity in heaven or we will be cast into hell—a place of eternal torment (Luke 16) 'into the fire that shall never be quenched' (Mark 9:43), a place from which there is no return. Between heaven and hell there is 'a huge chasm that cannot be bridged' (Luke 16:26, TPT). That means a decision must be made here on earth. There is no sitting on the fence or delaying the decision until a future time. Bearing all that in mind, it is impossible not to consider your role as a parent in raising your child not just in the things of God but to ensure they know the truth.

To add to that fear, adolescence and early adulthood can for many people bring the 'attitude of being too powerful to be defeated by anything', or feelings of being 'invincible', 'unshakeable', or even 'immortal'. For others, they think they have a lifetime ahead of them and can delay the decision over where they will spend eternity. This can lead to your child taking risks and getting involved in things which puts their life and others unnecessarily in danger. This type of behaviour sadly is not limited to children and adolescents, adults are also guilty of it.

Trying not to be fearful over the path down which your prodigal child is going, can be difficult. Somehow it seems justifiable and right to be concerned but also to fear that you are completely powerless as a parent to do anything about it. At times you could easily be convinced that your child has pressed a self-destruct button. Everything within you wants to stop them in their tracks and protect them from the inevitable consequences of sin and the wages it pays out, but you cannot. In fact, nothing you say or do would make a difference. If anything, it would drive them further away. As the parent of a prodigal child [regardless of their age], your fears may be heightened that some harm will come to them, or their life will be cut short and they will not have the opportunity to get themselves right with God.

Another fear that may enter your head surrounds the topical discussion about free will. Although each of us does have a free will and are responsible for our own decisions, we may fear that our prodigal child will use their free will and choose not to follow God. Miller and Miller Juliani (1997), in their book 'Come back Barbara', had fears that their child was someone who was an 'apostate or indeed that they become a reprobate or.... [were] never destined to be a child of God' (p. 48). You too may have similar fears. Or you may be afraid that by choosing not to follow God, your child will waste the life He gave them. Ultimately, time and the years will slip by and when God returns and your child stands before Him giving an account of their life, and the talents He gave them, they will not have lived it in the way they should. Therefore, God will reject them and heaven will not be their eternal destination.

In response to this period in your life where fears and anxieties are running rampant in your head, you may have embarked on a ferocious pursuit of answers to your many questions, possibly on the sovereignty of God. Undertaking such a search may have taken you in many different yet diverse directions. Depending on where you looked or what you found, this will either have exacerbated your fears or helped alleviate them.

Having a fear of the future, what it holds and what change may look like, seem perfectly justifiable given the circumstances you find yourself in and the fact that you do not know the end outcome. Those fears can arise at any time through a variety of triggers. You may be fearful that your relationship with your child will never be what it was or should be again. Or, you may be fearful that your child will get involved with the wrong partner in life. For other parents, fears exist because they thought their child's path in life would take a certain route but instead, it is going in the opposite direction. Alternatively, you may be afraid that your child will follow in your footsteps and make the same mistakes you or someone else in your family made. Arguably all these fears are only natural. We fear the things we cannot control or the situations we have no blueprints for.

Such fear and anxiety will make you want to change the situation you are in to reduce the amount of uneasiness you are feeling and experiencing.

Another fear may exist around your specific role in bringing about change in the situation with your prodigal child. It would be easy to fall into the mindset that for things to change, somehow you had to, for example, pray for a certain number of hours, or read so many chapters of the Bible each day. Failure to do so, would therefore mean you are personally responsible for not bringing about change in the life of your prodigal child.

Powerful weapons against fear

The list of fears could go on and on but it is time to stop and pause that rollercoaster of thoughts. Your head will be bursting and your heart will be so very heavy under the weight of it all. Take a moment. Breathe. Start to reflect back over your own life. Think about God's faithfulness to you and how His hand protected your life so many times and only allowed you to go so far and no further. Then ask yourself 'why is it so difficult to believe that the situation is any different for my prodigal child?' Doing so 'will reinforce your confidence that God will take you [and your prodigal child] through the next battle just as He has seen you through past difficulties' (Omartian, 2008, p. 67).

Proverbs 16 tells us clearly that 'A man's heart plans his way, but the Lord directs his steps' (v9). Only God knows the plans He has for you and your prodigal child. He knows which circumstances are necessary in your life and that of your child's, to produce the results and make you both into the people He intends you to be (Bridges, 1993). You can definitely trust God to guide you and your prodigal child in the plans and purposes He has. The Psalmist says 'He leads me in the paths of righteousness for His name's sake' (Psalm 23:3). God is leading you and your prodigal child. It may not seem like it or even look like it but He says He is and He cannot lie.

We talked previously about faith being the antidote to fear and about putting on the garment of praise when we feel the spirit of heaviness.

We have also talked about God giving us songs in the night, anthems for the 'dark night of the soul', where fear, worry and anxiety prowl around (Giglio, 2017). Rejoicing and praising God may seem like an avoidance tactic, a diversion, or blocking out the reality and seriousness of what is happening. Your parental instincts will battle against the idea of rejoicing and praising God under such circumstances. They tell you that this situation is real, it is critical and you have every right to be worried, anxious and fearful. God is not asking you to rejoice because of the situation you find yourself in or that your child has gone into the far country. Remember, we are told to rejoice 'because we believe He is in control of those circumstances and is at work through them for our ultimate good.... we are to look beyond our adversity to what God is doing in our lives and rejoice in the certainty that He is at work in us to cause us to grow' (Bridges, 1993, p. 175).

God holds your future in His hands and He will help you overcome your fears and challenges. The outcome of your storm, fiery trial and the waiting season is not dependent on the roll of a dice or some statistical theory or pattern. As you look at your situation, you can confidently say 'with man this is impossible but with God all things are possible'. Short-circuiting the pain and anguish you are going through will definitely seem like an attractive plan. But what you may fail to recognise and accept is that God wants to take you through it rather than take you out of it. He says, 'I will go before you and make the crooked places straight; I will break in pieces the gates of bronze and cut the bars of iron. I will give you the treasures of darkness and hidden riches of secret places, that you may know that I, the Lord, who call you by your name, Am the God of Israel' (Isaiah 45:2-3).

Throughout this book, I have tried to provide you with encouraging words but also give you practical steps to help you learn on your journey of 'Being the parent of a prodigal child'. No matter what stage you are at, think about some of the previous situations and fears you have had and write them down. Then beside them, write down the outcome of that situation, the lessons you learned and some of the ways God orchestrated and maneuvered things to turn it all around for your good. Not only will you start to see the ways that God undertook for you in the past but your focus and thinking will shift. You will remember the faithfulness of God in your previous situations and if God took you through them, He can and will do it again. On reflection, your current situation will not seem so impossible any more.

Another point to note is that earthly logic does not apply in storms, fiery trials or during the waiting season. So rather than focusing on what is going on with your prodigal child and trying to work things out yourself, start concentrating on your relationship and walk with God. Meditating on His word will build and strengthen your faith for the situation you find yourself in. By entering into the work God has planned for your life you will stop being steered by a spirit of fear but will instead, start to feel empowered by a spirit of love (Conlon, 2012). 'God has not given us a spirit of fear, but of power and of love and of a sound mind' (2 Timothy 1:7). You and your prodigal child are not just numbers, you are both important to God. His promises are greater than anything man could even begin to predict. When satan, or indeed other people, tell you to give up or that your situation is hopeless and not going to change, stand firm in your faith and keep moving forward, step-by-step. Remember that each time your faith is tested, you will develop perseverance which then leads to your character maturing in the things of God.

Learning to wait on God is not an easy thing to do but you need to be close to the heart of God to hear what He is saying to you. God is ready and waiting to meet, listen and talk to you. He wants to give you peace and hope in the midst of the chaos going on. There is only one voice amongst all other voices that is able to change your situation and lead you in the direction you need to go. You need to clearly discern the voice of God and allow yourself to be directed by the truth rather than the lies and fears satan would try to weigh you down with.

As you begin to hear the voice of God more clearly, He will begin revealing His word to you just as He promised He would in Isaiah 30, 'Your ears shall hear a word behind you saying 'This is the way, walk in it, whenever you turn to the right hand, or whenever you turn to the left'' (vs. 21). 'Failure to hear and obey the voice of the Lord is the spring from which all fears emerge' (Conlon, 2012, p. 15). If you choose to embrace God's will for your life, you will be surprised and overwhelmed at the journey He will take you on, the things He will reveal and the doors He will open for you.

You do not have to be a slave to fear. That is exactly what satan is trying to do to you. If he can weigh you down in fears and anxieties you will become powerless to help yourself or your prodigal child. Satan knows the power of a praying parent and is trying to take you out of the game completely. Do not succumb nor give in to his tactics. Boldly declare the words of this song, 'I'm no longer a slave to fear, I am a child of God.... My fears are drowned in perfect love'.[xvii]

Prayer is one of the strongest weapons we have in our toolkit against fear, yet sadly it is one of the first things we stop doing when circumstances get tough. How tempting it is to then draw back from situations in fear and trepidation because they look so big and seem completely impossible to personally handle or overcome. Time and time again we fail to remember that God does not want us to rely on own strengths. Stories in the Bible show us that God did not want His people then either to rely on their own skills, abilities, volume of numbers [men/soldiers], weapons, or any other human resources they had. Rather, He seemed pleased when His people were weaker than the enemies they faced in order that He could reveal and demonstrate His mighty power through the victories and battles they won.

Fear not

There are so many wonderful 'fear not' verses of scripture in the Bible. Some of these include—'Fear not, for I am with thee' (Genesis 26:24, KJV); 'Fear ye not, stand still and see the salvation of the Lord' (Exodus 14:13, KJV); 'Fear not, for I am with you; be not dismayed, for I am your God. I will strengthen you' (Isaiah 41:10).

One of the most beautiful but heartbreaking 'fear not' verses in the Bible is in Genesis 21. You may remember the story—ten years had passed since the promise that God would make Abram's descendants as innumerable as the stars. However, Sarai had still not borne any children and she had given up all hope and expectations of ever having a child herself. Unbelief had either overtaken Sarai or her faith had not yet fully developed. Either way, it would seem she had forgotten about God's mighty power to fulfil His promises. Her impatience at the delay to the promise led to her taking matters into her own hands. So, she decided to create a plan of her own to obtain an heir and went ahead with this plan without first seeking counsel of the Lord.

Sarai's plan was to give her Egyptian maidservant Hagar, to her husband in the hope she would bear him children. Hagar was possibly given to Abram by the king of Egypt some years before (Henry, 1992). Using a surrogate mother was acceptable and practical to the culture at that time. In Bible days, a man could also have a concubine(s) even though he was already married. A concubine was a woman who cohabited with a man but she could not marry her master because of her 'maidservant status'. Concubines would therefore have a lower position in the household than that of a wife. However, Sarai's plan was not for Hagar to be Abram's concubine, she was to become his wife. Hagar would therefore hold the same position in the household as Sarai, but with the caveat that she was to continue with her maidservant duties.

When Hagar realised she was pregnant, she began to look scornfully at her mistress. She started to boast of the fact that she was bringing an heir to Abram and thought 'herself a better woman than Sarai, more favoured by heaven and likely to be better beloved by Abram' (Henry, 1992, p. 42). Therefore, she would not submit to Sarai as she had done in the past. Sarai suffered dearly for her actions and plan to try and force God's promise to come to pass. It was an emotional price Sarai paid whereby the hatred, pride, arrogance, humiliation and belittling of her, by Hagar, became unbearable. Sarai handled the situation by dealing so harshly with Hagar that she ran away.

This passage is the first in the scriptures to mention the appearance of an angel. Verse 7 says 'now the angel of the Lord found her [Hagar] by a spring of water in the wilderness, by the spring on the way to Shur' (Genesis 16). Given that Shur lay towards Egypt, it would look as though Hagar was making her way back towards her home country. Going back to Egypt would have meant returning to their gods, not to mention the dangers in the wilderness through which she would have had to travel. God met Hagar not just in a physical wilderness but in a personal one. He spoke directly into Hagar's life and situation and gave her enough information about the future to enable her to take the next step. God told her, 'Go home, and humble thyself for what thou hast done amiss, and beg pardon, and resolve for the future to behave thyself better' (Henry, 1992, p. 42). He also told her that she was going to have a baby boy and his name was to be called Ishmael, which means 'God hears'. Ishmael would be 'a wild man. His hand shall be against every man, and every man's hand against him. And he shall dwell in the presence of all his brethren' (Genesis 16:12).

Hagar did return and remained with Abram and Sarai for the next fourteen years, during which time Issac was born. Then one day Sarai [now Sarah], saw Ishmael scoffing or poking fun at Issac. Once more she spoke to Abram [now Abraham] and this time told him to send Hagar and Ishmael away because she did not want him to be an heir with Issac. Reluctantly, Abraham agreed and so Hagar and Ishmael departed and wandered in the Wilderness of Beersheba.

Hagar's situation and the outcome for herself and her son seemed to have reached a place of no return. Although she had in the past, been mean to Sarah, there is no doubt she loved her son. The pain of losing him to the heat of the desert was unbearable but she could see no alternative other than a bleak future ahead especially as the water skin Abraham gave them had dried up. We read, 'Then she went and sat down across from him at a distance of about a bowshot for she said to herself, 'Let me not see the death of the boy'. So, she sat opposite him, and lifted her voice and wept' (Genesis 21:16). The word 'wept' in this verse means to 'weep bitterly'. Verse 17 tells us that God spoke and said 'What ails you Hagar? Fear not, for God has heard the voice of the lad where he is. Arise, lift up the lad and hold him with your hand for I will make him a great nation. Then God opened her eyes, and she saw a well of water. And she went and filled the skin with water, and gave the lad a drink' (Genesis 21:17-19).

Hagar was physically exhausted with the walking and the heat of the wilderness but she was also blinded by a fear of the future. When God spoke to her, he gave her two commands. Firstly, 'fear not', secondly, He called her to action, 'arise' or stand up. He heard the cry of her heart for her son and stepped in at just the right time whilst also meeting her physical need of water. Then He gave her a promise and a ray of hope that she could hold on to for the future. Once again, God revealed and demonstrated His mighty power to this mother even though she must have felt very alone, vulnerable and at the weakest and lowest point in her life.

As we come to the end of Chapter 8, there are so many lessons we can learn from Hagar's story. Namely, no matter what your situation is, it is time for you to arise and keep going knowing that you are powered by the promises of God for your life and that of your prodigal child's. God is able to save no matter how calamitous and hopeless your situation looks. The limitless ability of God which He has available for His people is mind blowing. But there are also actions placed on you. You need to read the word of God, hear His voice, lean on the promises and be reminded again that He has a plan for your life and your prodigal child's. Believing matters!

God is bigger than whatever fear satan would try to weigh you down with. Most importantly, God wants to lead and guide you through your storms, fiery trials and during the waiting seasons of your life just as much as He does when you are having a mountaintop experience.

Chapter 9

Divine interruptions

'When my anxious thoughts multiply within me, Your comforts delight me'.

(Psalm 94:19, AMP)

We allow ourselves to become so busy in ministry and serving God with whatever skills, talents and interests we have. Every day is crammed full and we genuinely believe we are faithfully serving God and following His will for our lives, and quite possibly we are. However, anything that interferes with that is assumed to be an interruption from the enemy—especially when it seems to be purposefully thwarting and keeping us back from what we are trying to do and achieve for God.

Our busy lives and church schedules do not have capacity for the minutest of interruptions let alone one so distracting, lengthy and time consuming as a child heading into the far country. If we are completely honest with ourselves, somewhere deep inside we may even quietly believe God could or should have prevented this from happening to us in the first place. After all, it is diverting our time and efforts away from the ministry and the work we are doing for Him!

What we fail to discern or recognise, is that it is actually a divine interruption from the Lord. It is also intended to bring about a divine reset in your life. If and when God changes your direction, that does not necessarily mean you were heading down the wrong road. What it does mean is that He wants to change the direction you are heading in to position and prepare you for what He has ahead (Omartian, 2008). Although we will have prayed and asked God many times for things to change, and for Him to draw us closer, this particular interruption does not fit with our expectations of what that should look like. Because of that, we do not embrace such interruptions as being from God. Instead we are quick to dismiss them as coming from the enemy.[22]

Many of you reading this book may be feeling battle weary and discouraged. What you are going through as the parent of a prodigal child is unquestionably difficult. In addition to that, it is hard to explain to other people the extent of the turmoil you are going through with being the parent of a prodigal child. Those who have not been through the same situation do not always fully understand. Despite having shed every tear that is left within you, breakthrough still seems so very far away, if not entirely impossible. Taunts and torments from the enemy keep coming and you find yourself going round in circles, caged and trapped in feelings of guilt and fear over decisions you have made, how you parented your child and things you could or should have done differently. Your faith may seem suffocated, all hope may have been suppressed and trust in God's promises is dimming with each passing day. Whispers from the enemy in your ear keep telling you God has let you down, you heard wrong and breakthrough is not coming.

After trying hard to deal with all the voices spinning round your head and endeavouring to stay focused on the word of God, there comes a point in time when you really just need to know that God is not absent in the midst of the chaos. You want to be reassured He sees your turmoil, the rollercoaster of emotions, the sorrow and the crippling pain you are experiencing. Inside there is a deep, deep longing to feel the nearness of God which will drive out your fears and give you the strength to take another step, and live another day.

---

22. https://lanavawser.com/i-heard-the-lord-say-i-am-interrupting-embrace-the-divine-interruptions-for-there-you-will-find-a-new-move-of-my-spirit-2/

The God who sees

In the last chapter, we only talked very briefly about Hagar but much more could have been said because there are so many lessons to be learned from her story. One of the noteworthy points I want to mention just now is about the conversation between Hagar and the Lord. You may have noticed that others in the scriptures refer to Hagar as: 'an Egyptian maidservant'; 'her maid'; 'my maid'; and 'your maid'. But when God addresses her, He personalises it. He calls her by name and even refers to the role she was playing at that time. 'Hagar, Sarai's maid, where have you come from, and where are you going' (Genesis 16:8).

God loved Hagar and He saw and knew the distress she was going through. After the conversation, Hagar was left in no doubt that her pain had been seen and recognised and so she calls the Lord 'El Roi' which means 'The God who sees me' (Genesis 16:13). Unlike other names for God in the Bible, this is the only time this particular name for God [El Roi] is used.

It is interesting to note that God did not initially take Hagar out of her difficult situation with Sarai. Rather, during the conversation, God told Hagar to return to Sarai and Abram. Strangely enough, nothing about Hagar's situation had actually changed to entice nor encourage her to go back to Sarai and Abram. The turning point was the conversation and personal encounter Hagar had with God who then directed her next steps.

Hagar was not the only person we read of in the Bible that God 'saw'. In John Chapter 1 we read about Nathanael who was a genuine, sincere, upright and Godly man. Nathanael was walking alongside Philip and as they drew closer, Jesus said 'Behold, an Israelite indeed, in whom there is no deceit'. Jesus commended Nathanael, not to flatter or puff him up, but because he was a genuine person. There was no deceit in him, he was sincere in his repentance for sin and sincere in his covenanting with God. While many others would be delighted at such a compliment from Jesus, Nathanael disregarded them because he was struggling with two things. Firstly, he wondered how Jesus knew so much about him. Secondly, his modesty or humility would not allow him to see himself worthy enough for Jesus to take notice of him. But Jesus did take notice and He knew everything about him. He knew Nathanael was a modest man—possibly edging on a melancholy man, someone who doubted his own sincerity. Jesus' comments to Nathanael were purposefully intended to put to rest the doubts Nathanael had about himself.

Nathanael asked Jesus 'How do you know me?' Jesus replied with a detailed, descriptive and accurate account of a specific moment in time which had personal significance and meaning to Nathanael. He said, 'Before Philip called you, when you were under the fig tree, I saw you' (John 1:48). It is most likely Nathanael would have been meditating, praying and in communion with God. 'Under the fig tree' in the Old Testament suggests being safe and at leisure. One commentator puts it beautifully 'when thou wast retired under the fig tree in thy garden, and thoughtest that no eye saw thee, I had my eye upon thee, and saw that which was very acceptable'.

Those fourteen words might not seem significant to you or me but they were to Nathanael and whatever he was doing that day under the fig tree, it was a private and intimate moment for him. Jesus' response to his question was therefore a pivotal turning point for him. What a beautiful picture of our Lord Jesus as He slowly and delicately revealed who He is to Nathanael. In comparison, Nathanael's response to Jesus feels like an outburst of an inward recognition and confirmation, 'Rabbi, You are the Son of God. You are the King of Israel' (vs. 49).

Just as Jesus knew all about Nathanael, He knows all about you and what you are going through. He is waiting on you and watching over your every step. Jesus knows the desires of your heart and the hidden fears buried within. He sees your deepest, innermost thoughts and prayers including the ones you cannot find the words to utter. As Proverbs 15 says, 'The eyes of the Lord are in every place, watching the evil and the good [in all their endeavours]' (vs. 3, AMP).

Showing empathy to someone who is going through a storm, fiery trial or who is in the waiting season is important but the cry of the brokenhearted seeks much more than that. It yearns for a specific and direct word regarding your situation but which also acknowledges where you have been, what you are going through, and provides direction for the future. When God speaks right into your situation as He did with Hagar and Nathanael, that is exactly what He does. Not only does that change everything, it also gives you strength and confidence to carry on. 'One word from His heart released into our lives can heal our hearts, break the chains, bring freedom, shift the atmosphere and bring life' (Vawser, 2018, p. 112).

An encounter with God

Throughout this book, I have mentioned a number of different practical steps to help you on your journey of being the parent of a prodigal child. By way of a quick recap, these include: waiting on the promises; hearing and recognising the voice of God; focusing on what God is doing; building your faith; pursuing God's heart; hearing His voice in the silence; persistence in breakthrough; and recognising the fears of your heart. In addition to these, what is most needed during difficult times is an encounter with God, but what difference is that likely to make in your life?

In trying to answer that question, the story that came to me is in Matthew's gospel. Chapter 27 tells us there were certain women who frequently followed Jesus' ministry and supported Him with whatever substance they had. Listed amongst these women is a lady called Mary Magdalene. The Bible does not give us a lot of information but she most likely has this name because she came from an area called Magdala which is located along the shores of the Sea of Galilee. The water springs, fertile land and fishing industry made it an important and prosperous village and region in Bible times. Ancient writings which mention Mary, refer to her as 'Mary the plaiter of hair'.

1 Timothy 2 tells us that the plaiting of hair was not viewed as modest apparel for women in Bible days. Mary is, however, most famously known as the person out of whom Jesus cast seven demons. Unlike Nathanael, we do not read about Mary's first encounter with Jesus. What we do know is that Mary's encounter with Jesus had a significant impact on her just like it did Nathanael's. So powerful must have been the encounter that it gave her back her life, a reason for living and arguably compelled and drove Mary [and the other women] to follow Jesus and faithfully support His ministry.

We should not underestimate the significance of what it meant to follow Jesus. He was constantly moving about, preaching, teaching and ministering. The sheer heat of the day, no home comforts, personal safety, exhaustion and possibly being away from family and friends, would have been a personal sacrifice and challenge for these women. We do not know what age Mary was, how fit and able she was or what family commitments she had. Neither do we know what it meant for her and the other women to follow Jesus and minister to Him.

Mary's journey with Jesus took her to the events of the cross. Mark 15 tells us 'There were also women looking on from afar, among whom were Mary Magdalene' (vs. 40). Mary saw first-hand what her Saviour went through for her and how He took her place on the cross. She knew she was the one worthy of death, not Him. Mary loved Him and served Him in life and here she is, loving and serving Him in His death on the cross. How Mary coped with the events leading up to and after Calvary is hard to fully comprehend. To see and hear what they did to her Saviour, the one she put so much effort into looking after, caring for and ministering to must have been unbearable.

Mary was also at the burial of the Lord Jesus. In a strange yet peculiar way—what a privilege but what a difficult task. Matthew 27:61 says 'And Mary Magdalene was there, and the other Mary, sitting opposite the tomb'. Since her encounter with Jesus, life had revolved and centred around following Jesus and ministering to Him and the disciples. If ever there was a time to question yourself and your purpose in life, Mary had every right at that time. What had all this been for? What was she going to do now?

Had Mary quit and not been faithful to the end, she would have missed out on a wonderful blessing. Mary had gone to the tomb early and while it was still dark. Other gospels say there were other women there with Mary but for some reason, John's gospel (Chapter 20) only records Mary as having gone to the tomb. Nonetheless, when she gets there, she sees the stone rolled away and eventually she picks up the courage to look inside. Mary thought no-one else noticed her as she stood there weeping. The beautiful part about this story is that while all this was going on, Jesus was watching her. It says 'she turned around and saw Jesus standing there' (John 20:14). He was there with her throughout it all and saw her tears. What an honour to be the first person to whom Jesus appeared to after conquering the keys of hell and of death (Mark 16, Revelation 1).

So many characters in the Bible such as Joseph and Nicodemus were asked or compelled to undertake incredible things. They took Jesus' body off the cross, handled the crown of thorns that had been put on His head, removed the nails that pierced His hands and feet, handled His back which the soldiers had whipped, saw His face which was marred more than any man, and dealt with His side which the soldiers had pierced. We do not often take the time, or sufficient time, to think about these things. Neither do we consider how powerful the encounter with Jesus must have been for the characters who came into contact with Him. The impact of it must surely have influenced them throughout their lives.

Encounters with Jesus are not limited to characters in the Bible. They are available to us today just as much as they were then. Our divine interruptions are further opportunities to draw close to Jesus and have that encounter with Him in new ways and on deeper levels which will also impact and influence our lives forever.

Finding purpose

Storms and fiery trials often come without warning and it can be really hard at the time to understand what is happening in your life and the purpose for such powerful yet divine interruptions. Up until now, we may consider that we have had a general idea of how our life and future is going to work out. And for a season it may look like everything is trundling along nicely in that direction, until of course, our plans are upset and interrupted. The way ahead then suddenly becomes cloudy, the picture is confused and it is impossible to figure out where you are and where you are going. Finding purpose in it all can be challenging.

I have asked God to show me clearly what He is doing in and through my life. He is so gracious that He has not only told me once, He has repeated it so that I get the message and keep getting it loud and clear. Let me give you an example. I recall speaking to a mentor I had for a course and being somewhat professionally frustrated because others seemed to be having an apparently easier time than me at undertaking a project we all had to do. I shared with her my well thought out analysis and comparisons on why I thought it was easier for them to undertake their projects as compared to mine. However, I will never forget her reply. She simply said, 'Yes, it is easier to implement a project like theirs, but at the end of the day, you will have learned the most and will be able to write more about the ways in which you overcame the obstacles and the challenges you encountered. It is those messages that others need to hear and will want to hear from you'. Although she was obviously talking about the course and the project, it made me think back to a word God had given me a couple of years prior through the ministry of Lana Vawser. Below is an abbreviated extract of just a few of the words which were relevant to me.

> 'God is training you in the midst of the battle to be an overcomer. You are actually receiving your next message for this season. You are walking out on what you are going to preach, write, sing and encourage others in. God is training you right now so that you will stand, be fortified and you will not be moved. The decree of God over your life is to arise and shine. He is perfecting you in your faith. He is maturing you, developing your character, strengthening your trust. God has you in the palm of His hand. He is bringing you out stronger than when you went in. He is extending you, maturing you and establishing you in faith. God is looking to reintroduce you to His power. Powerful testimonies will come forth that says 'only God did this'.
>
> You are not alone in this battle. God is breathing upon your life right now in such a powerful way. You will never be the same, you will be completely changed by what God is doing in your life. That is why the enemy is trying to take you out. Don't you dare give up. Do what God is calling you to do. You will be so overtaken by the revelation of Jesus Christ and who He is. God is saying 'stand strong, renew your mind, hold onto my hand because I am overtaking you with my purpose, my passion, my heart and my word like never before'. Go deep with Jesus. Be real. Open your heart to Him' (Vawser, 2019[23]).

---

23. https://youtu.be/q0SwF7e2LZM

Divine interruptions

I believe God divinely interrupted my life and has allowed me to walk out what I would write about in this book and encourage others wherever I go. That is, I believe, the purpose in all this. I hope that through my obedience in following what I believe God has asked me to do, this book will in turn achieve the fullness of what God planned it for and that it will reach those for whom He intended it to be written.

I have learned so much on this journey of 'Being the parent of a prodigal child' and it is all credit to the person of the Holy Spirit who has taught me. These lessons would not have been learned had God not divinely interrupted me. Life without storms, fiery trials and the waiting season definitely seems like a much easier path but just as a good painting and tapestry needs light and dark tones to turn it into a masterpiece, so too do we. There is a poem called 'The Weaver' which so perfectly captures this message.

'My life is but a weaving
Between my Lord and me
I cannot choose the colours
He worketh steadily

Ofttimes He weaveth sorrow
And I in foolish pride
Forget He sees the upper
And I the underside

Not till the loom is silent
And the shuttles cease to fly
Shall God unroll the canvas
And explain the reason why

The dark threads are as needful
In the Weaver's skillful hand
As the threads of gold and silver
In the pattern He has planned'.

(Author unknown)

It is time to change how you are viewing the divine interruptions in your life and think about the lessons God is trying to teach you. While it may be hard at the start to understand the full extent of what God is doing, you can be confident in knowing that He is able to do what He said He would do. It is not your role to figure out how it will all work together for your good. Your role is to be obedient and follow what He has asked you to do. Then you need to leave the who, when, where and how, up to Him. Gradually, the picture will begin to form and shape together like pieces of a jigsaw.

The journey ahead will undoubtedly require you to be empowered and strengthened. One way to do that is to stand firm on the promises of God and refuse to move from them. Discerning the times, the seasons and what the voice of God is saying to you, in this situation, is key to helping you arise out of the ashes stronger than you were before and awakened to the power of the Holy Spirit. Do not submit to the tactics and tricks of satan nor give credence to his attempts to intimidate, dishearten and wear you down. Ask God to give you strength to endure and rebound. Let hope arise even though you are being tested.

It is time to push through the noise, the chaos, the voices and look forward and upwards to Jesus. Shake off the heaviness and weights that are trying to hold you down by getting into the word of God, His presence and praising Him. Take God at His word. He is faithful and His promises will come to pass because His word cannot and will not fail. All of this has not been for no reason. The purpose will eventually become clearer and God will be glorified in and through it all.

Psalm 46 encourages us to hope and trust in God, His power and in His providence. There is nothing in your life that is out of God's control and no-body can take you out of the Father's hand. Keeping Jesus at the centre of your focus and heart will prevent you from being moved by the hardship of the times you find yourself in. As a Christian, you can have an inner peace which only comes from God and it will not make sense to the world. Following Jesus gives you the opportunity to show the stability that God can give to those who choose to put their trust in Him. Place your confidence firmly in God, build upon the rock, trust in God and be amazed at what He will do with but also in and through your life.

Do not be discouraged when you do not feel like you are a victorious overcomer walking on the mountaintop during storms, fiery trials and during the waiting season. It does not mean that your faith is weak or failing. Strong winds will rage during a storm and you will find it hard to do anything other than stand still and pray. Needless to say, the power of prayer and fasting, should not be undermined. They are powerful weapons which limit satan. 'Prayer is a unique gift from God to those who believe in Him. It is the most powerful force on the earth. The power of prayer lies not in the prayer but in God who stands at the other end of our cry. Prayer is the channel by which God's mercies are welcomed on the earth. It receives and welcomes heaven's help, heaven's life and heaven's rule on the earth and into our lives' (O'Higgins, 2016, p. 35).

This is also a good time to remind yourself that God is not the only one that has a plan for your life. Luke 22 in The Passion Translation says 'satan has obtained permission to come and sift you all like wheat and test your faith. But I have prayed for you.... that you would stay faithful to me no matter what comes' (vs. 31-32). During that sifting process, sometimes all you can do is to once more stand still and pray. God has a good and right plan for your life and He is working all things together for you. However, satan would endeavour to counteract that plan by taking away your praise, faith, hope, boldness, faithfulness and your confidence in God. Although it may seem ineffective, the shifting and shaking process separates the impurities and begins to position you. For that reason, it is possible to have joy during difficult times because your focus is fixed on Jesus and you know He is going through it with you and there is a reason and purpose for it all.

As mentioned previously in this chapter, there are other names in the Bible for God and one of these is El Shaddai. Although there are different interpretations for El Shaddai, a common one is 'The Overpowerer' which means 'God will do what He purposes to do, overpowering all opposition'. Another potential meaning of El Shaddai is 'The God of the mountain'.[24] Being the parent of a prodigal child may feel similar

---

24. https://www.biblestudytools.com/bible-study/topical-studies/what-is-the-meaning-of-the-name-shaddai.html

to climbing a mountain. But God can move the mountains in your life no matter how challenging and impossible they appear. Nothing is too difficult for Him.

Wherever He leads

Following Jesus wherever He leads you will not be easy. The work He wants to do in and through your life requires you to undergo certain processes, none of which can be speeded up. Neither are there any shortcuts. Becoming impatient particularly when situations are uncomfortable or do not change quickly enough, can happen very quickly. The journey and following God obediently through the storms, fiery trials, the waiting season and the unknown is an integral and indispensable part of the preparation process for what lies ahead for you. Experiences along your journey will increase and stretch your faith, refine your character and equip you for greater challenges in the future. Throughout each storm and trial, your patience is being developed, doubts and fears are being confronted and conquered, and your relationship with God is growing and deepening. Although the struggle is very real, as well as painful, difficult and uncomfortable, it is a necessary part of the journey and your preparation process.

Yielding to the Spirit of God and following His plan sounds easier than having to make the plan up from scratch for yourself but needless to say, it is not that simple. However, God has set before you an open door and going through it will be worth it all. Along the journey, He will show you things to come but it will test your faith and confidence. Hold on to God's promise to you in Psalm 30 which says 'weeping may endure for a night, but joy comes in the morning' (vs. 5).

Conclusion

This has been an incredible journey and not one I imagined I would ever have to tread. Nonetheless, the lessons I have learned will hopefully inspire and help you in your journey of 'Being the parent of a prodigal child'. If there is one last piece of advice I can pass on to you it would be to make a conscious decision not to give up. Stand in the gap for your prodigal child, they are depending on your prayers. satan has come to steel, kill and destroy their life but God has come that your prodigal child might have life and life more abundantly (John 10). Everything may not all come together the way you thought it would but it will all work together for your good. Be encouraged by Jeremiah 31 which says:

'Refrain thy voice from weeping, and thine eyes from tears: for thy work shall be rewarded, saith the Lord; and they shall come again from the land of the enemy. And there is hope in thine end, saith the Lord, that thy children shall come again to their own border' (vs. 16-17, KJV).

I know from experience that the persistent ranging winds will question your ability and desire to keep persevering. And as mentioned before, there will be many days where you feel that God has asked too much of you. The Passion Translation of 1 Corinthians 10 says 'We all experience times of testing, which is normal for every human being. But God will be faithful to you. He will screen and filter the severity, nature, and timing of every test or trial you face so that you can bear it. And each test is an opportunity to trust Him more, for along with every trial God has provided for you a way of escape that will bring you out of it victoriously' (vs. 13).

So how do you keep going and persist during such times? Pastor James McConnell of the Metropolitan Tabernacle Whitewell used to say, 'just keep loving Him'. You may not know what to say, where to turn, or what to do but just keep loving Him. Sometimes the only words I have been able to say are 'Lord You have my heart. Lord you know my heart. Please help me and show me what you are doing in this season. Give me the strength and direction to take the next step in the plan You have for my life'.

There is a famous quote by Alan Redpath who was a well-known British Evangelist, Pastor and author. He said 'There is nothing, no circumstance, no trouble, no testing that can ever touch me until, first of all, it has gone past God and past Christ right through to me. If it has come that far, it has come with a great purpose, which I may not understand at the moment. But as I refuse to become panicky, as I lift up my eyes to Him and accept it as coming from the throne of God for some great purpose of blessing to my own heart, no sorrow will ever disturb me, no circumstance will cause me to fret, for I shall rest in the joy of what my Lord is. That is the rest of victory!'.[25]

It has been said before throughout this book, the situation you find yourself in has not taken God by surprise. If He led you into the storm, fiery trial or the waiting season then He will lead you through and out of it again. This book started with the story of the prodigal son in Luke 15 and about the father [parent] being left at home during the time the prodigal is in the far country. Both the elder and younger brother in the passage underestimated the love and grace that the father had for them. Similarly, your Heavenly Father loves you and your prodigal child, no matter what.

The prodigal was slow to realise the extent of his father's love and that it was permanent and not based or predicated on any condition(s). While in the far country, the prodigal son knew enough about his father to know that he would be accepted when he returned. The welcome, however, was far more than he could ever have hoped or imagined. The transformation and return of the prodigal son was, and still is, a reason for the father [parent] to celebrate. God's grace and faithfulness to His word and promises is always more than we could ever expect or indeed, what we deserve. I will leave you with the words of one final song from Elevation Worship[xviii] which says it all.

---

25. https://www.azquotes.com/author/24224-Alan_Redpath

Worthy is Your Name

'It was my cross You bore
So I could live in the freedom You died for
And now my life is Yours
And I will sing of Your goodness forevermore

Chorus

Worthy is Your name, Jesus
You deserve the praise
Worthy is Your name

And now my shame is gone
I stand amazed in Your love undeniable
Your grace goes on and on
And I will sing of Your goodness forevermore

Be exalted now in the heavens
As Your glory fills this place
You alone deserve our praise
You're the name above all names'.

Further Reading

Bowen, B. M. (1944), *Strange Scriptures that Perplex the Western Mind*. Cambridge. Wm. B. Eerdmans Publishing Company.

Brannen, J. and O'Brien M. (1996), *Children in Families*. Bristol. The Falmer Press.

Bridges, J. (1993), *Trusting God even when life hurts*. Colorado Springs. NavPress.

Carothers, M. (2012), *Amazing power of faith*. California. Merlin R. Carothers.

Conlon, C. (2012), *Fear not*. California. Regal.

Conlon, C. (2013), *Unshakable. Trusting God when all else fails*. Minnesota. Bethany House Publishers.

Conlon, C. (2018), *It's time to pray. God's power changes everything*. Florida. GPC Books.

Dillow, L. (2007), *Calm My Anxious Heart*. Colorado Springs. NavPress.

Dixon, F. W. (1976), *Great and Mighty Things. Words of Life* paperback No. 3. London. Cox and Wyman Ltd.

Dixon, F. W. (1978), *Elijah's God and Mine*. Bucks. Hunt Barnard Printing Ltd.

Dunn, R. (2005), *Don't just sit there… have faith*. Bucks. Authentic Media.

Durkin, K. (1995), *Developmental Social Psychology: From Infancy to Old Age*. Chapter 3, pp. 77-110: 'Attachment to Others' Oxford. Blackwell Publishers.

Gass, B. (2005), *The Word for Today*. Volume III. Florida. Synergy Publishers.

George, E. (2008), *Walking with the Women of the Bible*. Oregon. Harvest House Publishers.

Giglio, L. (2017), *Goliath Must Fall. Winning the battle against your giants*. Tennessee. W. Publishing Group.

Harvey, E. F. and L. (2007), *Kneeling We Triumph*. Indiana. Old Paths Tract Society.

Henry, M. (1992), *Matthew Henry's Commentary on the Whole Bible*. Massachusetts. Hendrickson Publishers Inc.

Holmes, J. (1993), 'Attachment, anxiety, Internal Working Models'. In *John Bowlby and Attachment Theory*. London. Routledge: pp. 61-85.

Hybels, B. (1997), *The God you're looking for*. Tennessee. Thomas Nelson Inc.

Knowles, V. (1998), 'Promise and Fulfilment: Believing the Promises of God'. *Leaven*, Vol. 6., Issue No. 3, Article 4.

Lazar, V. (2017), *Amazing Grace: An Autobiography*. Dascalu-Ilfov. Magna Gratia Ministries.

MacArthur, J. F. (1985), *The MacArthur New Testament Commentary: Matthew 1-7*. Chicago. The Moody Bible Institute.

Martin, B. (1965), *John Newton and the Slave Trade*. London. Longmans, Green and Co. Ltd.

Mearns, D. and Thorne B. (2007), *Person-centred Counselling in Action*. 3rd Edition. London. Sage Publications Ltd.

Miller, C. J. and Miller Juliani, B. (1997), *Come Back, Barbara*. New Jersey. P. & R. Publishing Company.

Nelson, T. (1997), *New King James Version Study Bible*. Nashville. Thomas Nelson Inc.

Nelson, T. (2018), *New King James Version Study Bible* (3rd Edition). Nashville. Thomas Nelson Inc.

O'Higgins, P. and N. (2016), *The Supernatural Habits of the Spirit Empowered Believer*. 3rd Edition. Stuart, Florida. Reconciliation Outreach Inc.

Omartian, S. (2000), *The Power of a Praying Parent*. Oregon. Harvest House Publishers.

Omartian, S. (2004), *The Power of Praying. Help for a Woman's journey through life*. Oregon. Harvest House Publishers.

Omartian, S. (2005), *The Prayer that changes Everything*. Oregon. Harvest House Publishers.

Omartian, S. (2008), *Just enough light for the step I'm on*. Oregon. Harvest House Publishers.

Omartian, S. (2008), *The Power of Praying through the Bible*. Oregon. Harvest House Publishers.

Omartian, S. (2012), *Lead me, Holy Spirit*. Oregon. Harvest House Publishers.

Roberson, D. (1999), *The Walk of the Spirit—The Walk of Power: The Vital Role of Praying in Tongues*. Tulsa. Dave Roberson Ministries.

Ruonala, K. (2015), *From Wilderness to Wonders*. Florida. Charisma House.

Schoenhals, G. R. (1990), *John Wesley's Commentary on the Bible*. Michigan. The Zondervan Corporation.

Sexton, C. (2001), *The Lord is My Shepherd. The Twenty-Third Psalm*. Tennessee. Crown Publications.

Sproul, R. C. (2018), *The Promise of God*. Colorado Springs, USA. David C. Cook.

Taylor, H. L. (1952), *Little Pilgrim's Progress*. Illinois. Moody Bible Institute of Chicago.

Tenney, T. (2003), *Finding Favour with the King*. Minnesota. Bethany House Publishers.

Unwin, M. (2016), *Eagles*. London. Bloomsbury Publishing.

Unwin, M. and Tipling D. (2018), *The Empire of the Eagle*. London. White Lion Publishing.

Vawser, L. (2017), *Desperately Deep*. Coolum Beach, Queensland. Lana Vawser Ministries.

Vawser, L. (2018), *The Prophetic Voice of God*. Shippensburg. Destiny Image Publishers Inc.

Vawser, L. (2020), *A Time to Selah*. Shippensberg. Destiny Image Publishers Inc.

White, A. (1952), *Bible Characters: The Old Testament*. Vol. 1. London. Lowe and Brydone (Printers) Ltd.

Songs

i. *With all I am* – Reuben Morgan. Hillsong Music Publishing Australia.
ii. *Oceans (Where feet may fail)* – Joel Houston, Matt Crocker, Salomon Lighthelm. Hillsong UNITED.
iii. *Sovereign Over Us* – Jack Mooring, Aaron Keyes and Bryan Brown. Capitol Records.
iv. *Live for Jesus* – Evie Tornquist Karlson and Pelle Karlsson.
v. *What a friend we have in Jesus* – Joseph Scriven.
vi. *Friend of God* – Israel Houghton and new Breed – Live from another level.
vii. *Another in the Fire* – Joel Houston, Chris Davenport. Hillsong United.
viii. *The Blessing* – Kari Jobe, Cody Carnes, Chris Brown and Steven Furtick.
ix. *Jesus (You are able)* – Ada Ehi.
x. *Goodness of God* – Jason Ingram, Brian Johnson, Ed Cash, Ben Fielding, Jenn Johnson. Bethel Music Publishing.
xi. *See A Victory* – Jason Ingram, Fen Fielding, Christopher Joel Brown, Steven Furtick. Elevation Worship.
xii. *Freedom* – Edward Goltsman, Kim Crawford. Jesus Culture.
xiii. *Worthy of it all* – David Brymer. Amblecote Christian, England.
xiv. *Do it Again* – Steven Furtick, Matt Redman, Mack Brock, Christ Brown. Elevation Worship.
xv. *There was Jesus* – Zach Williams, Jonathan Smith and Casey Beathard.
xvi. *Hope Has a Name* – Aaron Johnson, Benjamin Cruse, Evan John and Ryan Williams. River Valley Worship.
xvii. *No Longer Slaves* – Joel Case, Jonathan David Helser, Brian Mark Johnson. Bethel Music.
xviii. *Worthy is Your name* – Chris Brown, Mack Brock and Steven Furtick. Elevation Worship.

www.ingramcontent.com/pod-product-compliance
Lightning Source LLC
Chambersburg PA
CBHW050357120526
44590CB00015B/1717